Comparative
Political
Ideologies

A. Phillips

Comparative Political Ideologies

MOSTAFA REJAI
Miami University, Ohio

St. Martin's Press

New York

Library of Congress Catalog Card Number: 83–61597
Copyright © 1984 by St. Martin's Press, Inc.
All Rights Reserved.
Manufactured in the United States of America.
87654
fedcba
For information, write St. Martin's Press, Inc.
175 Fifth Avenue, New York, NY 10010

cover design: Darby Downey
text design: Darby Downey

cloth ISBN: 0–312–15358–9
paper ISBN: 0–312–15359–7

To The Memory of
THOMAS P. JENKIN
Master Teacher and Consummate Scholar

About the Author

Mostafa Rejai received his Ph.D. from the University of California at Los Angeles and is now Distinguished Professor at Miami University (Ohio), where he has also been the recipient of an Outstanding Teaching Award. He is coauthor (with Kay Phillips) of *World Revolutionary Leaders* (1983) and *Leaders of Revolution* (1979) and author of *The Comparative Study of Revolutionary Strategy* (1977) and *The Strategy of Political Revolution* (1973). Professor Rejai is editor of and contributor to *Decline of Ideology* (1971) and *Democracy: The Contemporary Theories* (1967). In addition, he has coauthored *Ideologies and Modern Politics* (1971, 1975, 1981), edited *Mao Tse-tung on Revolution and War* (1969, 1970), and contributed to *Perspectives on World Politics* (1981), *Handbook of Political Conflict: Theory and Research* (1980), *The Theory and Practice of International Relations* (1974, 1979), *Dictionary of the History of Ideas* (1973), and *The New Communisms* (1969). He has been an associate editor of the *Journal of Political and Military Sociology* since its founding in 1973. His articles have appeared in social sciences and humanities journals in the United States and Europe.

Preface

This short book has three interrelated objectives. First, it sets out to develop a framework for the comparative analysis of political ideologies. Second, it examines some of the most prominent political ideologies of our times. Finally, it applies the framework to the ideologies discussed.

The first task is undertaken in Part I (Chapter 1), wherein five interconnected dimensions, or components, of ideologies are identified and elaborated. These are the cognitive, the affective, the evaluative, the programmatic, and the social-base dimensions. The chapter also briefly discusses the rise of ideologies and the functions they perform.

The second task is the subject of Part II (Chapters 2–7). There, six ideologies are analyzed and evaluated. As is readily apparent, I am highly selective about the ideologies I treat. Rather than bombarding the reader with a dozen or more ideologies, I have chosen the six *most significant* or *explosive* political ideologies of the nineteenth and twentieth centuries: nationalism, fascism/nazism, Marxism, Leninism, Maoism, and democracy. Leninism and Maoism, needless to say, are variations upon Marxism (or so it is claimed); as such, absolute precision would have required that the chapter on Lenin be labeled Marxism-Leninism and the one on Mao, Marxism-Leninism-Maoism. However, since the contents make this point abundantly clear, I use the shorter labels in the interest of brevity and symmetry. (Considerable thought was devoted to including a chapter on democratic socialism, but this ideology has been losing vitality in recent decades and today is simply not in the same "league" as the others. Nonetheless, the topic is discussed in the chapter on democracy.) In all instances, I should make explicit, I am interested in analyzing and understanding political ideologies *as ideologies* and not in the politics or governments of the countries in which these political doctrines may be found. Each of the ideology chapters closes by analyzing the ideology in terms of the analytical framework of Chapter 1.

I return to this matter, the third objective, in Part III (Chapter 8). There, the entire discussion is recapitulated by comparing the six ideologies in the light of the analytical framework. The central objective is to sharpen our focus and improve our understanding of political ideologies in general. The reader may wish to apply the framework to other ideologies as well; I have found the effort quite feasible and fruitful.

An analytical framework, I should note, has no intrinsic value. Rather, it is valuable only to the extent to which it provides a useful tool for the analysis of a particular phenomenon and, in so doing, helps sharpen our understanding of that phenomenon. It is in this light that the reader should judge the framework proposed in Chapter 1 and carried through the balance of the book. To this topic I return in the concluding chapter.

No chapter, I should stress, claims to be definitive or comprehensive. Rather, each represents *my* particular approach to or treatment of the subject matter. Alternative approaches and orientations will be found in the representative bibliography included at the end of each chapter.

The book concludes with two appendixes. Appendix A deals with some important distinctions between political ideology and its two brethren, political theory and political philosophy. Appendix B presents a brief discussion of the topic of "decline (or end) of ideology." These topics are important in their own right and provide potential materials for further study and class discussion. But since they are somewhat technical and abstract, I have placed them at the end of the book so as not to risk discouraging the uninitiated reader.

This book assumes no prior knowledge of ideologies and should be readily accessible to all undergraduate students. The treatment is straightforward and relatively brief, covering the most essential points and excluding much detail. Consequently instructors will have room to draw on their expertise to augment the ideologies discussed as well as to introduce others, while students will be able to explore the topics further on their own. I have deliberately avoided formal footnotes throughout in the hope of improving the text's flow and readability.

Comparative Political Ideologies may be used in a variety of courses. It can serve as a primary text in courses in political ideologies and political thought and as a supplementary text in political theory, comparative politics, international politics, and American politics.

I have tried to be as "objective" as possible and to keep my own ideological predilections from creeping into the text. It is only safe to assume, however, that I have not entirely succeeded. After all, there is no such thing as a totally scientific or "value-free" discussion of any subject, least of all ideologies. Let me put my cards on the table, as it were, by stating that while operating within the broad framework of a democratic ideology, on some issues and policies I lean to the right, on others to the left, and on still others to the center.

My deep gratitude goes to nearly a generation of Miami students and to my Miami colleagues for continuing intellectual nourishment and stimulation. More specifically, I am indebted to my colleague Warren L. Mason; to reviewers Robert A. Gorman of the University of Tennessee, Terence Ball of the University of Minnesota, Willard E. Smith of the University of Wisconsin–Oshkosh, Isaac Kramnick of Cornell University, Max B. Thatcher of the University of Connecticut, and to a sixth, who preferred to remain anonymous; and to Michael Weber of St. Martin's Press for offering many comments and criticisms. I much appreciate the patience and good humor that Dorothy S. Pierson brought to the typing of the successive drafts of the manuscript. Finally, I am grateful to Richard Steins and Carol Ewig of St. Martin's Press for skillfully steering the manuscript through production and to Joanne Ainsworth for a superb job of copyediting.

In closing, I would be grateful for any reader reactions (whether faculty or students) to this text. All criticisms and suggestions—whether negative or positive, substantive or procedural, interpretive or factual—would be deeply appreciated.

Mostafa Rejai
Oxford, Ohio

Contents

xiii

PART III   RECAPITULATION

APPENDIXES

PART I
COMPARATIVE FRAMEWORK

1

Comparative Analysis of Political Ideologies

Any effort at adequate analysis of political ideologies is contingent upon a clear understanding of (1) what ideologies are, (2) when and how they historically arose, and (3) what functions they perform for individuals, societies, and governments. These three interrelated issues constitute the subject of this chapter. A clarification of the first issue, as we shall see, is particularly helpful for developing a framework for comparative analysis of political ideologies.

THE NATURE OF IDEOLOGIES

Definitions of ideology are legion. Some writers emphasize the sociological components of ideology, others its psychological characteristics, and still others its psychocultural features. No one definition is intrinsically better than any other. The acid test is utility in scholarly discourse. The superiority of one definition over another lies in the extent to which it provides a more adequate, more searching, more powerful explanation of the phenomenon at hand.

Any adequate conception of ideology must meet certain explicit criteria. It must be neutral rather than pejorative. It must be reasonably precise without being unduly restrictive. And it must be, at least in principle, operational—that is,

3

applicable to the "real world." Rather than merely setting down a definition of ideology, I will try to identify and disentangle its major dimensions or components. This done, perhaps we will be in a better position to pull together the loose ends into a coherent framework for analyzing—and comparing—political ideologies.

The concept of ideology embraces five important dimensions:

1. cognition: knowledge and belief
2. affect: feelings and emotions
3. valuation: norms and judgments
4. program: plans and actions
5. social base: supporting groups and collectivities

Three clarifications are in order before we proceed to consider each dimension in turn. To begin with, the first three dimensions are adapted from the sociologist Talcott Parsons's conception of culture. Moreover, the five components are not mutually exclusive—that is, although analytically distinct, they overlap to some extent. Finally, all ideologies share these five components but to a lesser or greater extent—that is, not all ideologies are equally strong in all dimensions.

The Cognitive Dimension

"Cognitive dimension" refers to an ideology's "world view"— its outlook on society and politics, its perception of social and political reality. This world view consists of elements of both fact and fiction, both knowledge and belief. The distinction is straightforward. Knowledge is subject to the rules of logic (for instance, internal consistency) and the tests of science (for example, replication and verification). Beliefs, on the other hand, are notions and attitudes about society and politics that are accepted on faith—without any necessary foundation in reality. To illustrate, whether a people are governed by majority rule is in principle verifiable; whether they belong to the "super race" is not. Stated differently, there is no necessary or complete congruence between ideology and reality.

Having called into question the cognitive truth value of ideology, I will take a small step further to suggest that ideologies embrace deliberate elements of distortion or myth. This, in fact, is one of the few points on which most writers on ideology agree. The myth may be a small one (for instance, President Lyndon Johnson's "Great Society") or a big one (for example, Karl Marx's "classless society"), but a myth is there nonetheless.

The myth in ideology is socially and historically conditioned. It communicates a fairly complex message in simplified form, which is a hallmark of all ideology. Successful communication of ideology and its myth(s) cannot take place except through simplification. Simplification, in turn, is accomplished most notably through the use of symbols. Whether linguistic (words or speech) or nonlinguistic (flags, insignia, documents, monuments, holidays, anthems), symbols capture large expanses of meaning in an economical fashion and communicate these meanings in an instantaneous way. Moreover, symbols bring ideas together and relate them in a coherent fashion, making them readily intelligible—and they provoke an emotional response.

The Affective Dimension

The discussion of myth and symbol brings into focus the second dimension of ideology, its emotive (that is, emotion-laden) content. This component is rather self-explanatory and does not require extended elaboration.

To stress the affective dimension of ideology is not, of course, to deny all rationality in political doctrines, nor is it to suggest that ideologies will not attempt to hide their affect behind a facade of "objectivity" and "science." It is simply to say that all belief systems include both reason and emotion and that the weight put on each varies from ideology to ideology.* Beliefs may be held with relative emotive weakness or

---

*Throughout this work, "doctrines," "belief systems," and "ideologies" are used interchangeably and for stylistic convenience. With the exception of Appendix A, "theory" is also occasionally used in the same vein.

relative emotive intensity, with low or high affect. Similarly, ideologies may be relatively open and flexible or relatively closed and rigid. Thus the ideologies of nazism and fascism constitute highly emotive, closed, and rigid belief systems. The ideology of communism combines strong elements of the rational with strong elements of the emotional. The ideologies of democracy are characterized, at least in principle, by openness, flexibility, and rationality. In short, regardless of the degree of intensity, a most distinctive feature of all ideologies is an appeal to human passion, an eliciting of emotive response.

The Evaluative Dimension

Ideologies embody normative elements. Specifically, ideologies make value judgments in two ways: negatively, by denouncing an existing system of social and political relationships; positively, by putting forth a set of norms according to which social and political reconstruction is to take place.

The criticism of existing society is undertaken, at least in part, through appeal to high-sounding moral principles. Moral outrage and indignation are indispensable to any ideology. The attack against existing society is presented, rationalized, justified, and dignified in the light of appeal to "higher" principles.

The positive values of an ideology revolve around such central norms as liberty, equality, fraternity, humanity, and the like. The normative propositions are characteristically presented as factual statements.

All ideologies propose to move toward a "good society," however defined. Some ideologies posit an ultimate value, a final good, a utopia. Marx's idea of a classless society is an apt illustration.

Ideologies, as we can see, contain statements concerning the allocation of scarce societal resources (for example, power and wealth). Such allocation naturally involves adjustments and compromises among conflicting interests and demands. It also entails questions of rulership, authority, and legitimacy.

In this context, political ideologies are systems of beliefs and values focused primarily on such questions as: By what criteria are conflicting values and interests to be adjusted? Who (what person, group, or institution) has the authority to play a role in such adjustments, and under what conditions? Under what circumstances is the legitimacy, or popular acceptability, of a regime called into question? Under what conditions should one regime be replaced by another?

The Programmatic Dimension

The values, goals, and objectives of ideology are embodied in a more or less comprehensive program of activities. Ideologies, as many have pointed out, are action-related systems of beliefs, norms, and ideas. Not only do they posit a set of values, they also seek to relate specific patterns of action to the realization of those values. This demand for consistency between principle and behavior also serves as the basis for imposition of ideological discipline and control.

The action and program of an ideology may be directed toward the maintenance and perpetuation of the status quo or, more characteristically, toward the transformation of the existing social order. The program of ideology will set forth, implicitly or explicitly, a hierarchy of values and objectives. It may even include a statement of priorities specifying immediate, intermediate, and ultimate goals. In the Communist ideology, for instance, the immediate goal is overthrow of the bourgeois regime; the intermediate goal, social and economic reconstruction; the ultimate goal, a classless society.

The Social-base Dimension

Ideologies are necessarily associated with social groups, classes, collectivities, or nations. Ideology, to be ideology, must have a mass base. It must be presented to the populace in such a way as to be readily understandable and, in this understanding, to elicit a commitment to action toward the realization of goals and objectives. As many have pointed out, ideologies are mobilized belief systems. In this context, one may wish to make a distinction between personal ideology and political ideology.

The mobilization function of ideology is impossible without organization. Indeed, organization is the link between belief and action. But organization does not evolve spontaneously. Nor is it put together by the masses. Organization is an elite concept and an elite function.

It is necessary to draw a distinction between ideology of the elites and ideology of the masses. Briefly, the belief system of the elites will tend to be comprehensive, articulate, and coherent; that of the masses, partial, inarticulate, and incoherent. Stated differently, elites are always in a position to give a comprehensive statement of what they believe and why they believe as they do. The masses typically lack this capacity.

The elite-mass distinction gives rise to some intriguing questions. To what extent do elites use ideologies to move their peoples toward higher goals and objectives? To what extent do ideologies serve as covers for personal ambitions and motives of elites? To what extent do elites use ideologies in order to manipulate and control the masses?

Although it is impossible to attempt blanket, categorical answers to these and related questions, the possibilities of manipulation and control are, of course, quite real and frequently present in all ideologies. The form and degree of manipulation, needless to say, will vary from ideology to ideology. Both would be more intense in extremist ideologies and less intense in moderate ones.

Summary

I have identified five principal dimensions of ideological belief systems and have discussed each in some detail. In so doing, I have proposed a framework for the analysis of political ideologies, either as individual phenomena or, more importantly, in a comparative context. The framework is applied specifically at the end of each chapter as well as in the concluding one.

At this point, a summary definition of political ideology will necessarily sacrifice the intricacies of the concept, and I would prefer to avoid one. Since this is not a realistic option, however, I offer the following conception of ideology as consistent with the foregoing analysis.

Political ideology is an emotion-laden, myth-saturated, action-related system of beliefs and values about people and society, legitimacy and authority, that is acquired to a large extent as a matter of faith and habit. The myths and values of ideology are communicated through symbols in a simplified, economical, and efficient manner. Ideological beliefs are more or less coherent, more or less articulate, more or less open to new evidence and information. Ideologies have a high potential for mass mobilization, manipulation, and control; in that sense, they are mobilized belief systems.

Before turning to an analysis of some specific political ideologies, I must address two related matters: the rise of ideologies and the functions they perform.

THE RISE OF IDEOLOGIES

Political ideologies as we know them today began to emerge in the nineteenth century. A host of changes, events, and developments coalesced to produce an environment highly conducive to the rise of political belief systems. This environment simply did not exist in the agrarian, absolutist, tradition-dominated context of the pre-nineteenth-century world.

To begin with, the French Revolution of 1789 shattered the foundations of traditional, aristocratic, monarchical politics and ushered in the age of mass political participation. Prior to the Revolution, politics was an affair of the nobility and the aristocracy; thereafter, it became a mass, popular affair as well. "Liberty, Equality, Fraternity" was not an accidental slogan of the French Revolution. The expanding middle-class ranks rose up in a democratic revolution against the regime of monarchical absolutism, an experience that was repeated in the course of the nineteenth and twentieth centuries in other countries as well.

As the nineteenth century progressed, the phenomenon of mass participation intensified and spread to the lower classes. Three factors played especially important parts in this process. First, the rise of trade unionism (as a concomitant of industrialization) improved the economic position of the working classes. Second, the growth of workers' (or labor) parties penetrated the parliamentary systems of European countries to incorporate political representatives from the lower classes. Third, the gradual extension of the franchise guaranteed, at least in principle, popular participation in politics in the fullest sense. In short, as the nineteenth century opened, the middle class had become involved in politics; as it drew to a close, the working class was so involved as well.

Having begun well before the nineteenth century, urbanization achieved new heights during this period. Urbanization means many things, of course. Important for our purposes is the pattern of population movement from the farms to the cities, from the hinterland to the urban centers. By concentrating populations in relatively small places, urbanization provided the mass base of ideologies and the primary ingredient of ideological movements.

When combined, the twin forces of urbanization and industrialization produced yet another significant consequence: the increasing complexity, compartmentalization, and depersonalization of human life. The ideas and ideals of community and face-to-face relationships were destroyed. In their place there appeared a growing sense of human impotence, uprootedness, anonymity, and alienation. The spiritual and emotional gap thereby created—which was also exacerbated by a growing trend toward secularization—called for a new source of cohesion, a new source of belongingness, a new source of security, a new faith. And ideologies, of course, fulfill these fundamental human needs by making isolated men and women parts of much larger wholes.

Finally, advances in technology—particularly communication and transportation—made possible the rapid dissemination of ideologies. Ideologies became mobile, as it were, crossing national and international boundaries with great ease.

FUNCTIONS OF IDEOLOGIES

Ideologies perform an array of important functions, whether for individuals, groups, or governments. Some of these functions, implicit in what has been said above, will be made explicit in the interest of a well-rounded treatment.

First, ideologies set forth standards of behavior. They provide rationales for our words and deeds, give order to our lives, and "explain" the ambiguities of the world around us.

Second, ideologies provide individual identity and a sense of belongingness, which, as we have seen, are particularly important in mass, urban, industrial societies. Ideologies counteract our anxieties and insecurities.

Third, ideologies serve to achieve social solidarity and cohesion. For one thing, they bind a group together and give it a sense of unity. For another, they rationalize and justify group goals, values, and objectives. In giving a group legitimacy and respectability, ideologies improve not only the group's self-image but its external image as well.

Fourth, ideologies engender optimism. They provide hope, promise, utopia, paradise. Such optimism, needless to say, is essential to human life and to the mass appeal of ideologies.

Fifth, ideologies serve to support and maintain a political regime or to challenge and destroy it. In this sense, we may distinguish between ideologies of status quo and ideologies of change, although ideologies may perform both functions at the same time. So, for instance, the ideology of communism seeks to destroy the existing order and replace it with an alternative one.

Finally, all ideologies serve as instruments for the manipulation and control of the people. A country's leaders are always in a position to dupe the masses, particularly in the light of contemporary advances in technologies of communication. The only questions are the regularity, extent, and intensity with which popular manipulation and control are exercised.

Selected Bibliography

Adorno, T. W. et al. *The Authoritarian Personality*. New York: Harper & Bros., 1950.

Apter, David E., ed. *Ideology and Discontent*. New York: Free Press, 1964.

Aron, Raymond. *The Opium of the Intellectuals*. New York: Norton, 1962.

Bell, Daniel. *The End of Ideology*. New York: Free Press, 1960.

Burns, James. "Political Ideology." In *A Guide to the Social Sciences,* edited by Norman MacKenzie. New York: Mentor Books, 1966.

Corbett, Patrick. *Ideologies*. New York: Harcourt, Brace & World, 1965.

Cox, Richard H., ed. *Ideology, Politics, and Political Theory*. Belmont, Calif.: Wadsworth, 1969.

Hacker, Andrew. *Political Theory: Philosophy, Ideology, Science*. New York: Macmillan, 1961.

Harris, Nigel. *Beliefs in Society: The Problem of Ideology*, London: C. A. Watts, 1968.

Jenkin, Thomas P. *The Study of Political Theory*. New York: Random House, 1955.

Lane, Robert E. *Political Ideology*. New York: Free Press, 1962.

Larrain, Jorge. *The Concept of Ideology*. Athens: University of Georgia Press, 1980.

Lichtheim, George. *The Concept of Ideology and Other Essays*. New York: Vintage Books, 1967.

Lipset, Seymour M. *Political Man: The Social Bases of Politics*. New York: Doubleday, 1960.

Loye, David. *The Leadership Passion: A Psychology of Ideology*. San Francisco: Jossey-Bass, 1977.

MacIver, Robert M. *The Web of Government*. 1947. Reprint. New York: Free Press, 1965.

Mannheim, Karl. *Ideology and Utopia*. New York: Harcourt, Brace, 1936.

Rejai, Mostafa, ed. *Decline of Ideology*. New York: Atherton Press, 1971.

———."Ideology." In *Dictionary of the History of Ideas*, edited by Philip P. Wiener. 4 vols. New York: Scribner, 1972.

Rokeach, Milton. *The Open and Closed Mind*. New York: Basic Books, 1960.

Sartori, Giovanni. "Politics, Ideology, and Belief Systems," *American Political Science Review,* 63 (June 1969), 398–411.

Selinger, Martin. *Ideology and Politics.* New York: Free Press, 1976.
Shklar, Judith N. *Political Theory and Ideology.* New York: Macmillan, 1966.
Waxman, Chaim I., ed. *The End of Ideology Debate.* New York: Funk & Wagnalls, 1968.

PART II
SELECTED IDEOLOGIES

2
Nationalism

This chapter has three limited objectives. It seeks to (1) clarify the meaning of nationalism and related concepts, (2) examine the Western experience with nationalism by focusing upon France and, in passing, other European countries, and (3) examine the Eastern expressions of nationalism, with particular reference to Africa.* The chapter closes by applying our analytical framework to the ideology of nationalism.

THE MEANING OF NATIONALISM

Nationalism is a group's awareness of its membership in a nation—potential or actual—and its desire to attain, enhance, and perpetuate the identity, prosperity, and power of that nation. The adequacy of this definition hinges on the meaning of "nation" and of "potential or actual."

I shall define "nation" as a relatively large group of people who *feel* they belong together by virtue of sharing in common any one or more of such traits as race, history, culture, language, and customs and traditions. As a matter of actual fact, none of these traits may exist, but the people must *believe*

---

*The choice of France is unavoidable: it was, in a real sense, the cradle of nationalism as we know it today. My own interests have determined the references to other European countries and the selection of Eastern nationalisms.

that they do. In short, nationalism, as any other ideology, contains elements of myth.

Nationalism as an ideology refers to a social, cultural, and psychological condition in which one's supreme loyalty is to one's nation. It involves a belief in the intrinsic superiority of one's own nation over all other nations.

Types of Nationalism

The nationalist ideology may seek to create a nation that does not presently exist or to increase the power and prestige of one that already does exist. I shall designate the process of nation building as *formative nationalism* and the process of nation aggrandizing as *prestige nationalism*. If the aggrandizement of one nation entails annexation or conquest of other peoples, then I shall call it *expansive nationalism*. Thus, for example, the peoples of many parts of Africa and Asia have been involved in formative nationalism, efforts to terminate foreign rule and establish their own nations; contemporary nationalism in France is of the prestige variety; the nationalism of Nazi Germany, with its aim of conquering and dominating other peoples, was expansive.

Nationalism and Imperialism

There is an intimate connection between nationalism and imperialism. Put briefly, imperialism (another word for expansive nationalism) is a species of which nationalism is the genus. While imperialism may take many forms—military, political, economic, cultural—its invariant characteristic is the domination and exploitation of one people by another, rationalized and justified in any number of ways.

Nation and State

Nation, it is clear, is not the same as state. The latter refers to an independent political unit, controlling a specific territory, with a sufficient concentration of power to maintain its identity and continuity. State, in other words, is primarily a political-legal concept, and nation is primarily a psychocultural one. As such, nations and states may exist independently of one another; a nation may exist without a state, a state may exist without a nation. When the two do coincide, the result is either a *nation-state* or a *state-nation,* depending on which came first. Thus, for instance, the emergence of national and cultural consciousness preceded the formation of the state in Germany, whereas in France the situation was reversed and the monarchical state preceded national consciousness. Similarly in the Eastern world, Israel may be viewed as a nation-state, whereas all formerly colonial countries of Africa and Asia are state-nations.

WESTERN NATIONALISM

Nationalism is a distinctive phenomenon of the nineteenth century; it began in a real sense with the French Revolution. Love of country, of course, has always existed, but a distinction should be made between nationalism and patriotism. People have always and everywhere demonstrated emotional attachment to their native lands. This attachment—patriotism—is not nearly as intense as nationalism; it is not a mental state charged with burning emotions; it does not have a mass character; it does not become the basis of social movements.

The Beginnings of Nationalism

The French Revolution destroyed the foundations of traditional society and introduced the age of mass, popular politics. Overnight, as it were, France became a nation; and the nation assumed responsibility for its citizens, demanding loyalty and devotion in return. The people, having claimed the nation as their own, set out to abolish the monarchy, dispossess the nobility, and confiscate church property.

The glorification of the people coincided with the growth of certain democratic ideas and sentiments. The slogan of the French Revolution, "Liberty, Equality, Fraternity," meant just that. The people were demanding new rights, including those of representation and participation in public affairs.

National honor, national self-determination, and national sovereignty were inescapable components of the doctrine of nationalism. Monarchy, tyranny, and absolutism would no longer be tolerated. Equally important, these democratic values were seen not as belonging to the French people alone but to all peoples and nations. The French saw as their special mission the task of spreading and propagating these values.

Inspired by the example of France, peoples throughout Europe were to rise and overthrow monarchy and tyranny. If they were unable or unwilling to embrace the values of the French Revolution, then the French people would take it upon themselves to accomplish this task for them—by force of arms, if necessary. From its beginnings, in other words, nationalism became associated with messianism (that is, a sense of mission), expansionism, imperialism, and war. In the name of nationalism and democracy, Napoleonic armies launched an ambitious policy of conquest across Europe.

Soon after the French Revolution, nationalism flourished throughout the Continent. In Italy, Germany, Spain, Russia, and elsewhere, it became a consuming force. Frightened by French expansionism, the peoples of Europe rallied around their own rulers and formed their own nationalist ideologies.

The Italian nationalist movement, for example, dates back to the 1820s. Giuseppe Mazzini (1805–1872), the foremost intellectual-activist of the day, founded an organization, Young Italy, as early as 1831. Italian independence did not come until 1870, however, when the French position in Italy had weakened. Similarly, after decades of nationalist struggle under the leadership of Prussia, Germany was founded in 1871, on the heels of a victorious war with France.

In short, war and conquest by one nation heightened national consciousness in other nations and intensified a uniform need for large-scale military establishments. This, according to some scholars, sums up the essential history of Europe in the nineteenth century.

Before turning to the twentieth century, we must pin down yet another significant aspect of French messianism: to insist on the civilizing and humanizing mission of any one country (that is, on the superiority of any one people) is to insist at the same time on the relative inferiority of all other peoples. Later—when Europeans confronted the peoples of their colonies—this attitude found reflection in the slogan "the white man's burden."

Nationalism in the Twentieth Century

For a decade or so after each world war, nationalism was in a state of decline in the Western world; it no longer seemed relevant or desirable. This decline continued through the Great Depression, as various European countries turned their attention to urgent domestic matters.

The Second World War, on the other hand, occasioned a most dramatic burst of nationalism. This nationalism was associated with aggressor countries—primarily Germany and Italy—whose ambitious schemes led to cataclysmic events and enormous waste of human and material resources. To cite but one illustration, Germany's perceived need for additional "living space" was an automatic prescription for a policy of conquest and brutality (see chapter 3).

The war left the European countries in a state of military and economic disintegration and facing the potential threat of Soviet expansionism. Their mutual aims and aspirations thus spurred a desire for military and economic cooperation, as symbolized in the North Atlantic Treaty Organization (NATO) and the European Economic Community (the Common Market). These and other organizations signaled a trend toward increasing international cooperation designed to meet common needs and solve common problems.

The decline of European nationalism did not last long. Its resurgence was dramatically symbolized in Charles de Gaulle, who emerged as the personification of the Fifth French Republic in 1958. Once again, declarations of French "prestige," "sovereignty," and "grandeur" echoed across the continents.

Postwar French nationalism represents a reaction against two compelling phenomena: the loss of French colonies and the predominance of American power on the European continent. Nationalist revolts in the colonies were particularly disillusioning to the French because they directly challenged the myth of French superiority in all spheres. Not prepared to come to terms with colonial nationalist movements, the French continued to entertain illusions in Indochina, Algeria, and elsewhere. Defeat after defeat finally drove home the point that the universal mission of France had come to an end. Disillusioned in its self-assigned mission abroad, France turned inward—to the task of revitalizing itself.

Revitalization meant, among other things, confronting U.S. military and economic dominance on the Continent. France had suffered abject defeat at the hands of Germany in World War II. The end of German occupation did not mean the end of French humiliation, however, for in the eyes of many French citizens, the United States quickly replaced Germany. Accordingly, only substantial economic growth, the development of nuclear power, and the end of reliance on American aid could serve to moderate the intensity of French nationalism.

Since its economy was weak in the years immediately following the war, France sought economic strength in union with other continental powers, particularly Germany. The French then turned to military matters. "The two hegemonies," as de Gaulle labeled the United States and the Soviet Union, could be challenged only if France had its own independent nuclear power. A *force de frappe* (nuclear striking force) would be sought at any price, for it symbolized France's resurgence as a superpower. Having reestablished France militarily, de Gaulle could now afford to undermine NATO and force the American military establishment out of France.

The most important consideration about French politics in the postwar period is that it was dominated for over two decades by the Gaullists (1958–1981). Riding the tide of nationalist sentiment, de Gaulle forged a massive parliamentary majority unprecedented in French politics. Although de Gaulle has been gone for some time, Gaullism clearly remains. To be sure, subsequent French presidents have not been the charismatic leader that Charles de Gaulle was, but the substance of Gaullist policies remained largely intact for nearly a quarter of a century.

The election of François Mitterrand (a democratic socialist) to the French presidency in 1981 may have broken the spell of de Gaulle. But since the election hinged primarily on domestic issues, most changes were effected or projected in the domestic arena. The essential direction of French foreign policy remained unchanged. When it comes to nationalism and national prestige, there is in practice (though not necessarily in theory) no significant difference between socialists, liberals, or conservatives.

EASTERN NATIONALISM

Primarily a twentieth-century phenomenon, Eastern nationalism took place, for the most part, in colonial areas; and it was, in large measure, a reaction against Western policies of imperialism and conquest.

The First Stage of Colonial Nationalism

At the turn of the century, colonial nationalism (more precisely, anticolonial nationalism) was virtually an unknown phenomenon. Anticolonial feelings and sentiments gradually began to emerge after World War I. India and China, for example, seriously challenged the imperialist powers. Colonial nationalism gained momentum and spread rapidly after World War II. Countries in Africa, Asia, and elsewhere confronted imperialism with national revolutionary movements. Within two decades, dozens of countries had attained independence. Membership in the United Nations jumped from fifty-one at its founding in 1946 to more than three times that many in the 1980s.

As variants of colonial nationalism, African nationalist movements share many characteristics with their counterparts elsewhere. Using independence as the watershed that it necessarily is, we can focus upon the characteristics of African nationalism before and after this event.

The basic objectives of colonial nationalism are to terminate foreign rule and to create in its place a state-nation on an equal footing with other sovereign states (formative nationalism). In this context, colonial nationalism differs in some respects from nineteenth-century Western nationalism. For one thing, Eastern nationalism is largely a reaction against the spread of Western imperialism. As such, at least in its initial stages, Eastern nationalism is a movement of protest and revolt, often violent. The doctrinal and attitudinal contents of colonial nationalism are largely negative, signifying an outrage against foreign control. Thus, Nehru is supposed to have said that Indian nationalism is an "anti-feeling." Anti-imperialism alone, then, appears to be sufficient as a unifying force.

Protest and violence also serve as psychological outlets for the expression of pent-up grievances and frustrations. Not only does violence serve to unify the natives and destroy the outsiders, some maintain, it also helps in the process of psychological rehabilitation of the colonial people. Stated differently, violence helps bring freedom to colonial peoples while at the same time restoring their sense of dignity and self-respect. (See, for example, Frantz Fanon's book, listed in the bibliography for this chapter.)

Whereas the initial phase of colonial nationalism is almost exclusively negative, the later phase witnesses self-conscious formulation and popularization of a positive nationalist ideology. Here extensive political organization is undertaken, persistent attempts at the politicization of the masses take place, and Western and native symbols, as appropriate, are employed to rally the masses around the movement. As political consciousness grows and as the nationalist movement gains momentum, the colonial regime eventually acknowledges the end of its days. Where foresight was exercised, as in many British colonies, a peaceful power transfer took place; where it was not, as in the Belgian Congo, rampant violence broke out.

A further distinguishing mark of Eastern nationalism lies in the extremely important role played by the intellectual elite. Intellectuals have played important roles in all nationalist movements, but in the colonial world nationalism has been almost exclusively their handiwork. Colonial intellectuals have, in fact, served as intermediaries between Western and Eastern cultures. As is well known, a great many nationalists of Africa and Asia were educated at British, French, and American universities.

Eastern nationalism, particularly in Africa, does not seem to require a "nation"—if by that term we mean a well-defined body of people with distinct racial, cultural, historical, and religious ties. Indeed, many scholars believe that in the strict sense there are no nations in Africa. The "national" boundaries of African countries represent above all the administrative convenience of the imperialist powers.

To return to an earlier terminology, we can see that in the Eastern world state-nations are the rule and nation-states the exception. This suggests that in studying colonial nationalism, assumptions of cultural and social homogeneity must be seriously modified. This difficulty notwithstanding, however, given the disruption of traditional society under the impact of Western ideas, given the appearance of an effective leadership group, given popular mobilization—given, in short, the necessary, social, political, and economic changes—nationalist movements are bound to gain momentum.

Colonial Nationalism after Independence

The postindependence stage is marked by important changes both within and outside the nationalist movement. Internally, the attainment of independence works to undermine the united front that had characterized the movement. Since the unifying focus—independence—has now been removed, conflicting interests, competing leaders, intergroup rivalries, and separatist tendencies surge to the fore. This is not to say that there are no separatist tendencies in the preindependence period, but that the attainment of self-rule vastly exacerbates them. As a result, nationalist leaders in many African states have insisted upon an authoritarian single-party political system as a means of maintaining unity and neutralizing competing forces and pressures.

Externally, the attainment of self-government means the emergence, within a short period of time, of a number of "sovereign," independent political entities. This development has entailed problems of relationships among the new African states and between these states and the rest of the world. The former set of relationships has been marked by competition and rivalry, quest for recognition by the major powers, membership in the United Nations, and related matters. At this point, in other words, formative nationalism is transformed into the prestige variety. As for the second group of relationships, many African states have adopted a posture of "neutralism" as a means of keeping superpower rivalry out of Africa.

A final development in postindependence nationalism relates to a set of problems surrounding the phenomenon of neocolonialism. Neocolonialism means that although an imperialist power has formally granted independence, it continues to maintain political, military, economic, and cultural ties with its former colony—and that through these ties, it continues the policies of domination and exploitation. Moreover, it is argued, neocolonialism is worse than colonialism because it is subtle and indirect and therefore not subject to any form of international control.

On the question of neocolonialism, two distinct views sum up the reaction of the African states. One view, held by the leaders of conservative countries, such as Liberia, is that relationships with the imperialist powers should be maintained because they are mutually beneficial. The other view, expressed by radical countries, such as Guinea, stresses the necessity of cutting all ties with the imperialist powers in an effort to return to the old days of innocence before those powers came to spoil the purity of Africa. In fact, as early as 1959 Guinean President Sekou Touré had written a book titled *Toward Full Re-Africanization* (see the bibliography).

THE FRAMEWORK APPLIED

As we have seen, the cognitive dimension of nationalism involves elements of knowledge (fact) as well as of belief (fiction). Western nationalism sees the world through the prism of "the best and the greatest," seeking to enhance a country's economic, political, military, diplomatic, and cultural status. In the East, nationalism typically begins with the experience and perception of oppression, exploitation, and humiliation under foreign regimes, which lead, in time, to demands for independence, sovereignty, and all the prestige trappings attached thereto. Both types of nationalism rest on the assumption of the relative superiority of one country and the relative inferiority of all others. The French, for example, are not the only people who believe in their cultural supremacy; many an African people have internalized and expressed similar beliefs.

The affective component of nationalism stresses the feeling of belongingness to a unique—because superior—group or nation. It follows, by definition, that every individual constituting the group is unique and superior as well. These feelings of unity, distinctiveness, and superiority are captured in such emotionally charged symbols as national flags, national anthems, and national holidays.

The affective ingredient of nationalism, which in part overlaps with the evaluative, is also well illustrated in the concepts of civilizing mission (France), white man's burden (Great Britain), and manifest destiny and divine ordination (the United States).

The evaluative dimension of Western nationalism is summed up in the French Declaration of the Rights of Man and Citizen (1790): glorification of people and nation, popular (rather than monarchical) sovereignty, individual rights and liberties. Other values include national pride, honor, and dignity, as well as collective welfare and security. In the Eastern experience, another aspect is added to this dimension. Colonial countries want not only independence and sovereignty, they also wish to "get even" with the colonizers by seeking revenge, righting historic injustices, and releasing pent-up psychological frustrations.

Historically, the programmatic component of nationalism has found three expressions: (1) formative nationalism—educating, organizing, and mobilizing a people to assert their unity, identity, and independence, (2) prestige nationalism—mobilizing a people to improve their status, welfare, and power, (3) expansive nationalism—mobilizing a people to aggrandize themselves by infringing upon the rights of another people. Thus, having become a "nation" overnight as it were, France set out to increase its power and prestige. In so doing, it violated the rights of the Germans, Italians, Spaniards, Russians, and others in a series of wars that dominated the nineteenth century. Similarly, having attained independence from Britain, the United States, under the presumably divine ordination of manifest destiny, set out to expand over the entire continent and cross the seas to take over not only Cuba and Puerto Rico but Hawaii and the Philippines as well. That the implementation of manifest destiny entailed conflict and war was treated as a matter of course and routine.

The social base of nationalism incorporates the entire population except, perhaps, the radical intellectuals (the internationalists), the poor, the indigent, and the uneducated. In such diverse, multiethnic societies as the United States, national unity is more difficult to achieve than in homogeneous lands. Even in the United States, however, there is an "umbrella ideology" that brings together peoples of various regions and nationalities—the Northerners and the Southerners, the Poles and the Irish—and identifies them as "Americans."

Selected Bibliography

Canadian Review of Studies in Nationalism, 1 (1974) through 11 (1984). Journal devoted to subject of nationalism.

Carr, E. H. *Nationalism and After.* New York: Macmillan, 1945.

Coleman, James S. "Nationalism in Tropical Africa." *American Political Science Review,* 48 (1954), 404–426.

———. *Nigeria: Background to Nationalism.* Berkeley: University of California Press, 1958.

Deutsch, Karl W. "The Growth of Nations: Some Recurrent Patterns of Political and Social Integration." *World Politics,* 5 (January 1953), 168–95.

———. "Nation and World." In *Contemporary Political Science,* edited by Ithiel de Sola Pool. New York: McGraw-Hill, 1967.

———. *Nationalism and Its Alternatives.* New York: Knopf, 1969.

———. *Nationalism and Social Communication.* 2nd ed. Cambridge, Mass.: MIT Press, 1966.

Deutsch, Karl W., and Richard L. Merritt. *Nationalism: An Interdisciplinary Bibliography.* Cambridge, Mass.: MIT Press, 1966.

Emerson, Rupert. *From Empire to Nation: The Rise to Self-Assertion of Asian and African Peoples.* Cambridge, Mass.: Harvard University Press, 1960.

Fanon, Frantz. *The Wretched of the Earth.* New York: Grove Press, 1968.

Hodgkin, Thomas. *Nationalism in Colonial Africa.* New York: New York University Press, 1967.

Kautsky, John H. *Political Change in the Underdeveloped Countries: Nationalism and Communism.* New York: Wiley, 1962.

Kedourie, Elie. *Nationalism.* New York: Praeger, 1960.

Kohn, Hans. *The Idea of Nationalism: A Study in Its Origins and Background.* New York: Macmillan, 1944.

———. *Nationalism: Its Meaning and History.* Princeton: Van Nostrand, 1955.

———. *Prophets and Peoples: Studies in Nineteenth Century Nationalism.* New York: Macmillan, 1957.

Memmi, Albert. *The Colonizer and the Colonized.* Boston: Beacon Press, 1967.

Rejai, Mostafa, and Cynthia H. Enloe. "Nation-States and State-Nations." *International Studies Quarterly,* 12 (June 1969), 140–158.

Schaar, John H. "The Case for Patriotism." In *American Review 17,* edited by Theodore Solotaroff. New York: Bantam Books, 1973.

Shafer, Boyd C. *Faces of Nationalism.* New York: Harcourt Brace Jovanovich, 1972.

Sigmund, Paul E., Jr., ed. *The Ideologies of the Developing Nations.* New York: Praeger, 1963.

Smith, Anthony D. S. *Nationalism in the Twentieth Century.* New York: New York University Press, 1979.

———. *Theories of Nationalism.* London: Buckworth, 1971.

Snyder, Louis L. *The Meaning of Nationalism.* New Brunswick, N.J.: Rutgers University Press, 1954.

————. The New Nationalism. Ithaca: Cornell University Press, 1968.

Touré, Sekou. Toward Full Re-Africanization. Paris: Présence Africaine, 1959.

Ward, Barbara. Nationalism and Ideology. New York: Norton, 1966.

3

Fascism and Nazism

The opening decades of the twentieth century witnessed the rise of totalitarian regimes in Russia (communism), Italy (fascism), and Germany (nazism). Although these regimes differ in many ways among themselves, Western scholars labeled them "totalitarian" because they have some features or attributes in common. After a discussion of the ideological foundations of fascism and nazism, we shall examine these commonalities and differences; but first let us look at the two principal leaders of fascism and nazism and the historical and societal contexts in which they emerged.

MUSSOLINI AND HIS TIMES

Benito Mussolini was born on July 29, 1883, near a small town in central Italy, the first of three children. His father, the local blacksmith, dabbled in socialist journalism, which left a strong impression on the young child. The family lived in small and dingy quarters and led a meager existence.

Unloved at home, the young Mussolini became rebellious, violent, and aggressive. He was transferred from school to school for stabbing classmates with his penknife and attacking his teachers. At the same time, however, he was sufficiently intelligent to pass his examinations. Eventually he obtained a teaching certificate and taught school for a time.

31

Mussolini, however, was not to remain a teacher for long. Restless and ambitious, he left Italy for Switzerland in 1902, in search of fortune and adventure. Instead, he found a drab life, moved from menial job to menial job, and engaged in acts of violence as a means of venting his anger and frustration.

Meanwhile, Mussolini managed to read widely in philosophy and literature, particularly the works of George W. F. Hegel (1770–1831), Friedrich W. Nietzsche (1844–1900), Georges Sorel (1847–1922), and others (see below). Highly eclectic in approach, he retained only those things that appealed to his temperament and outlook. Though he had not formed anything approaching a philosophy of his own, he impressed others with his knowledge. He began to develop a reputation as a journalist, orator, and radical activist. Advocating violence and strikes as the means of improving the condition of the workers, he was arrested and imprisoned several times. By the time he returned to Italy in 1904, he had begun to make a name for himself.

After a period of relative inactivity, Mussolini returned to journalism, trade unionism, activism, and oratory in 1909. During World War I, he experienced frontline fighting and later became one of the most popular war correspondents. Soon thereafter these experiences and his intense reading of German nationalist literature and philosophy combined to effect a sharp ideological conversion. He had witnessed the middle-class fear of communism and he believed he had felt the pulse of the Italian people: his socialist tendencies gave way to intense nationalism. He became convinced that he was called upon to lead Italy to a new age of glory and vitality— indeed, to revive the great Roman Empire. "Viva l'Italia" became his rallying cry.

In 1919, a small and disparate group of individuals—republicans, nationalists, socialists, anarchists, unemployed former soldiers—came together in Milan to form what Mussolini called Fasci Italiani di Combattimento: a group of fighters united by close emotional bonds. So was born fascism in Italy—and so emerged Mussolini as Il Duce, the supreme and unchallenged leader.

A restless figure and always onstage, Mussolini launched a

campaign of mass mobilization throughout Italy, traveling from place to place, holding rally after rally, drawing ever-larger crowds, and mesmerizing listeners with his oratory stressing national greatness. Meanwhile squads of his Blackshirts unleashed a campaign of violence against all opponents, particularly the Socialists and the Communists.*

In the summer of 1922, at the gathering of a large group of Fascist supporters, Mussolini cried for a "March on Rome" as a means of usurping political power. Word spread, and all over the country Fascists seemed prepared to march. Sufficiently impressed and alarmed, King Victor Emmanuel III invited Mussolini to become prime minister. Assuming office in October, Mussolini remained in power for more than twenty years. In 1932, he teamed with his comrade Giovanni Gentile to write the definitive article "The Doctrine of Fascism," which glorified the state and outlined the social and political programs of the Fascist party.

HITLER AND HIS TIMES

Adolf Hitler was born on April 20, 1889, in a border town in Austria. His father, a minor government official, was an autocratic drunkard who paid little attention to family matters. The young Hitler, in turn, became moody, stubborn, and rebellious. The father died in 1903 but left sufficient money in savings and pension to keep the family in relative comfort.

For lack of acceptable grades, Hitler never completed secondary school. He aspired to become an art student but was twice denied admission to the Academy of Fine Arts in Vienna. Angry and disillusioned, he lived a drifter's life in his late teens and early twenties, sustaining himself on demeaning and menial jobs.

Hitler moved to Munich in 1913 and enlisted in the German army soon after the outbreak of World War I. Decorated twice for bravery, he found military life much to his liking—

---

*Fascist supporters wore black shirts as a means of identification and as a demonstration of solidarity and strength.

particularly the camaraderie, discipline, hierarchy, and potential for heroic deeds. At the same time, he became embittered at the German defeat and considered the peace settlements unacceptable.

In 1919, Hitler joined the German Workers' party in Munich (the political heart of conservative Bavaria), which organization was renamed the following year the National Socialist German Workers' Party (Nationalsozialistische Deutsche Arbeiterpartei, "Nazi" being a contraction of the first word). He found the party lacking in effective leadership, organization, discipline, a coherent ideology, and an ability to mobilize the people by capitalizing on their frustration and discontent. Germany of the 1920s and 1930s was in the grip of acute political instability and economic problems, including unemployment and depression. The humiliation of their defeat in the war lingered, and the resentment of the people increased.

Through his commanding personality, his oratorical skills, and his unceasing propaganda, Hitler set out to address Germany's political and economic problems and to restore to the German people their sense of national pride and integrity. Like Mussolini, he was a mesmerizing and spellbinding performer. Having assumed the leadership of the party in 1921, Hitler continued to draw larger and larger crowds. Patterned after Mussolini's Blackshirts, the Nazi Brownshirts, or Stormtroopers, were originally organized to provide protection for party leaders and party meetings; later, they were put to other, violent, purposes as well.*

In November 1923, Hitler participated in the unsuccessful Munich putsch (revolt or uprising), as a consequence of which he was sentenced to five years in prison. He served less than one year and he used the time to write the chief document of Nazi ideology, *Mein Kampf* (My Struggle), a rambling work in which he gave expression to the ideas of racism, expansionism, the leadership principle, the "folkish" state, and the like.

---

*Hitler had been an admirer of Mussolini, though at first Mussolini did not reciprocate. In fact, during their first meeting in the mid-1930s, Mussolini developed a very low opinion of Hitler. Only repeated demonstrations of German military might during World War II changed Mussolini's mind.

The economic crash of 1929 provided a fresh boost for the fortunes of the Nazi party. The unceasing and skillful manipulation of the Nazi leaders attracted people in huge numbers. "Germany, Germany, Germany" had become Hitler's perpetual battle cry. By the election of 1930, the Nazis had become the second largest party in Germany.

In 1932, Hitler ran for the presidency of the German Republic against Paul von Hindenburg. A military hero of World War I, Field Marshal von Hindenburg had been persuaded to enter politics by some conservative parties and became president in 1925. He managed to prevail over Hitler in 1932, but the Nazis captured a staggering seventeen million votes (44 percent of the electorate) and emerged as a most significant political force. In recognition of this fact, von Hindenburg appointed Hitler chancellor in 1933.

Once in office, Hitler moved swiftly to consolidate power and remove all opposition. The Reichstag (the lower house) fire of February 1933 (apparently set by a Dutch Communist) became a rationalization for a decree severely curtailing all freedoms, eliminating or nazifying the media, revamping the educational system, erecting concentration camps, and launching a campaign of violence against all opponents, especially Marxists, Communists, and Jews (whom Hitler blamed as the root cause of German problems). In March, Hitler maneuvered the Reichstag to pass an enabling act giving him full powers. After von Hindenburg's death in August 1934, Hitler moved to monopolize all power by merging the offices of the chancellorship and the presidency, the latter carrying the supreme command of the armed forces as well.

In 1936, Hitler formed an alliance with Mussolini. And the world stood on the brink of apocalypse.

WHY MUSSOLINI AND HITLER ATTAINED POWER

Given the sociohistorical contexts of Italy and Germany of the 1920s and 1930s, Mussolini and Hitler gained power for several identifiable reasons. First, their political doctrines were well in tune with the cultural and philosophical climate of the times—particularly the teachings of such towering figures as Hegel and Nietzsche, which had penetrated virtually all intellectual circles. Second, Mussolini and Hitler promised economic and political stability—indeed, unprecedented progress—in the midst of national crisis, turbulence, and chaos. Third, they mobilized their respective peoples by appealing to their grievances, frustration, and discontent—in particular the acute fear of communism among the middle classes. Fourth, Mussolini and Hitler promised to replace the humiliation of defeat with a new age of national pride and glory. Fifth, they used their "charismatic" personalities and superb oratorical skills to maximum advantage. Finally, Mussolini and Hitler offered strong leadership at a time when the Italian and German peoples seemed to crave it and when national consolidation seemed the most urgent need. In short, Mussolini and Hitler were children of their circumstances, and they responded to those circumstances with uncommon effectiveness.

IDEOLOGICAL FOUNDATIONS OF FASCISM AND NAZISM

Irrationalism and Activism

Fascism and nazism systematically downgraded the role of reason, logic, and intelligence in human behavior, stressing instead its irrational and emotional components. Life, according to these ideologies, defies rational explanation. Truth is elusive and ordinary minds are incapable of understanding anything in depth. What is needed is intuition, instinct, and emotion as the means of mobilizing and binding the masses. What is also needed is *action:* the simple and unambiguous assertion of one's power, force, and strength against all perceived corruption and evil. In a chaotic universe only the superior *will* can prevail. Political action—particularly of a violent nature—has value in and of itself: it is an exhibition of one's strength, an imposition of one's will, a demonstration of one's superiority. Violent action, in a word, is its own justification.

The ideas of irrationalism and activism drew heavily on a school of thought known as Social Darwinism, which sought to apply the teachings of Charles Darwin (1809–1882) to human society, national and international. Darwin had argued that the ability of organisms to adapt and survive depends on the possession of certain characteristics that makes them most suitable to their environments, and that this adaptation in turn leads to a process of "natural selection." Misinterpreting Darwin, the Social Darwinists (for instance, the Englishman Herbert Spencer, [1820–1903]) saw the world in terms of an "open struggle," in which there is "natural selection" leading to the "survival of the fittest." Both within and between nations, they maintained, it is the struggle for survival that leads to the selection of the best. The implications of Social Darwinism for racism and expansionism are rather clear, and they will be briefly discussed in the following section.

The ideas of irrationalism and activism also drew on the work of the French thinker Georges Sorel, who had stressed the importance of developing and propagating a social myth as a means of accomplishing one's objectives. Sorel's particular concern was the myth of the general strike as a means of improving the condition of the workers. Myth, according to Sorel, has no necessary foundation in reality; it is simply a statement of determination to undertake violent action, an emotional force inspiring and mobilizing the masses. Mussolini's "March on Rome" may well have been an expression of the Sorelian myth.

Nationalism, Racism, and Expansionism

Among the most prominent myths of fascism and nazism were those of nationalism, racism, and expansionism. The word *fasciare* means to bind or unite—and Mussolini sought to unite the people of Italy in search of a transcendent goal, namely, the revival of the glory of ancient Rome. Similarly, the two words *national* and *sozialistische* had been combined by some German intellectuals in the early part of the twentieth century in an effort to incorporate the working classes into a harmonious nationalist and democratic state, thereby overcoming the Marxist doctrine of class struggle (see chapters 4 through 6). Hitler used (or misused) "national socialism" as a means of uniting and aggrandizing Germany at the expense of all "inferior" nations and peoples.

Racism was more a characteristic of nazism than of fascism. Strongly influencing Hitler were the writings of the Frenchman Arthur de Gobineau (1816–1882) and the Germanized Englishman Houston Stewart Chamberlain (1855–1927). These writers distinguished between the white, yellow, and black races, stressing the superiority of the first. Within the white race, they distinguished between the Semites (presumably a combination of white and black races), the Slavs (presumably a combination of white and yellow races), and the Aryans (presumably the pure white race). Thus generated, Hitler quickly embraced the myth of Aryan supremacy because it justified both anti-Semitism and expansionism.

Within a nation, it follows, being superior to Slavs and Semites, the Aryan race should subjugate—even eliminate— the former in the interest of racial purity.* Similarly, *between* nations, the Aryans are superior to all others and hence justified in subduing and conquering them. Consistent with Social Darwinism, conquest and victory in war were seen as concrete manifestations of national vitality and superiority. This expansionism was formally justified in the Nazi concept of *Lebensraum:* the perceived need for more "living space."

As for fascism, Mussolini's commitment to the idea of the superiority of the Italian people may have had an underlying racial rationale, but the idea was not openly and blatantly racist. Although Mussolini at times appealed to racial themes, these themes appeared to rest on cultural (not biological) foundations.

By the mid-1930s, Mussolini did come to adopt an anti-Semitic posture, but most likely he did so in order to ensure full alliance with Germany. While introducing anti-Semitic

---

*Anti-Semitism had another root as well: according to a popular interpretation of the times, Germany lost World War I not because of the superiority of its external enemies but because of the betrayal and treachery of some internal elements, the Jews, particularly, and the Marxists.

legislation, however, he quietly deplored the brazen racism of Hitler. And he had severe misgivings about the polarization that the race issue introduced in Fascist party circles.

Party and State

The irrationalism and emotionalism of fascism and nazism found expression in their glorification of the party and the state as well. Relying heavily on Hegelian philosophy, the Fascists considered the state as the embodiment of all that is morally, spiritually, and materially valuable. In fact, Mussolini equated fascism with a theory of the state. Hence, in "The Doctrine of Fascism" we read: "Everything is the State and nothing human or spiritual exists outside the State."

Such a state, it follows, monopolizes all power and authority. It becomes a gigantic corporation swallowing and controlling all other aspects of society: economy, industry, labor, capital, family, school, church, peer group—nothing is outside its grasp. The "corporate state" is the protector of individuals, their rights, their welfare, their security: it makes individuals what they are. Hence, there can be no rights or freedoms apart from the state. Individuals find freedom and fulfillment only in total submission to the state. Individuals, groups, nation, state—all constitute one integral whole.

Relying on another German philosopher, Johann von Herder (1744–1803), the Nazis fashioned the concept of the "folkish (*völkisch*) state," stressing the peculiar, primeval, racial qualities of the German people. The folkish state is an organic whole protecting, preserving, enhancing, and glorifying the quintessential traits of the Aryans—a "higher humanity," Hitler called them. Racism, in a word, became a definitional component of the Nazi state and nation.

The principal agent making possible the realization and fulfillment of the Fascist and Nazi states is the political party. The party is the supreme—indeed, the only—organization; all other parties and groups are outlawed, the media are silenced, freedoms are revoked. The party functions as the link between (1) the leader and the cadre (middle- and lower-level officials), (2) the leader and the rank and file, and (3) the leader and the general public.

The party is the sole decision-making organism. And in order to implement its decisions, special methods may be used. Such was the rationalization for the formation of such paramilitary units as Mussolini's Blackshirts and Hitler's *Sturmabteilungen* (the SA, the stormtrooper division) and *Schutzstaffeln* (the SS, an elite guard and special police force).

Leader

The supreme person presiding over and guiding the state and the party was the leader: "Der Führer" in the case of Hitler; "Il Duce," of Mussolini. Hitler and Mussolini were in fact depicted as the very personifications of their respective nations. They were seen as having superhuman qualities of will, drive, ambition, vision, wisdom, and moral judgment. They supposedly possessed mystical gifts that enabled them to lead their countries toward ever higher goals. Their heroic deeds and actions, in turn, called for total quiescence on the part of their peoples.

The Fascist doctrine of leadership was heavily influenced by the work of Vilfredo Pareto, (1848–1923) and Gaetano Mosca (1858–1941). Known as the "elitists," these writers argued, in general terms, that human society at all times has been characterized by a minority that rules and a majority that is ruled—that is, elite and mass. They interpreted politics in terms of violent conflicts among contending elites for the ruling positions in society, which conflicts, in turn, produce a constant "circulation of elites"—that is, one group overturning another. In this historical process, ordinary human beings are simply materials to be manipulated, duped, and used for elite goals and objectives.

The Nazi concept of leadership (*Führerprinzip*) drew on the ideas of Nietzsche and Richard Wagner (1813–1883), who glorified the great deeds of superhuman and all-conquering heroes. Leadership qualities, they maintained, are always inborn, not cultivated. Only a few possess these qualities, and they alone are in a position to compete for the top leadership roles. In the process, some are destroyed, the best prevail. The ultimate arbiters are will, power, force. And hence we come full circle back to the doctrines of irrationalism and activism.

"TOTALITARIANISM"—RIGHT AND LEFT

The word "totalitarianism" is of relatively recent origin. First used to describe Fascist Italy and Nazi Germany, the term was later broadened to include all Communist countries as well. Although differing in many ways among themselves (some theoretical, some practical), these regimes are labeled totalitarian because they have some things in common.

Commonalities

Scholars have analyzed totalitarianism in various ways, but the two central and interrelated features of totalitarian regimes are a particular type of ideology and a particular type of organization. In essence, the totalitarian ideology is all-comprehensive, all-pervasive, rigid, and inflexible. It is mystical, magical, and claims infallibility. It is intolerant, demands total conformity, and seeks total control.

More particularly, totalitarian ideology has three identifiable components. First, it begins by criticizing and rejecting the existing order as corrupt and immoral. It denounces the existing system through appeals to higher norms and principles. Second, totalitarian ideology proposes an alternative vision of a better, superior society. The alternative order typically embodies a utopian vision, a grand myth—for instance, racial supremacy, classless society—which becomes a rallying cry for the masses. Third, totalitarian ideology embodies a statement of plans and programs intended to realize the alternative order. It seeks to relate specific patterns of action to the realization of values and visions. These components, it will be recalled, are found in all ideologies. What distinguishes totalitarian ideology is the fanaticism and extremism with which these components are stated and pursued.

The demand for conformity and control is assured by the second major component of totalitarianism: organization. Totalitarian societies are strictly hierarchical, compartmentalized, organized from top to bottom. Dominated usually by one man, *political* organization (the party) reaches out from the center and penetrates the entire country through regional, provincial, and local levels. *Social* organization is perpetuated by youth groups, professional groups, cultural groups, sports groups, and the like. Government and military bureaucracies, respectively, are emplaced in *civil* and *military* organizations. *Paramilitary* organization is pervasive in the form of the secret police. *Information* is effectively monopolized through the control of all media of communication: television, radio, the press.

As can be seen, totalitarianism seeks *total* control of all aspects of society, and thus it differs from such older concepts as despotism, dictatorship, or tyranny. For one thing, dictatorship seeks limited—typically political—control. Totalitarianism seeks "total" control: political, social, economic, religious. For another, totalitarian regimes are, at least initially, mass mobilization regimes: significant portions of the population actively identify with the movements. In contrast, dictatorships seek only pacified and submissive populations. Finally, totalitarian regimes seek complete *reconstruction* of man and society. Dictatorships attempt simply to rule over man and society.

Differences

Scholars have distinguished two types of totalitarianism: that of the right (nazism and fascism) and of the left (communism). Although they share the ideological and organizational features discussed above, the two differ in some respects. Right totalitarianism has been associated with relatively advanced societies (Germany, Italy), left totalitarianism with relatively undeveloped countries (Russia, China). This difference in turn is related to the social base of totalitarianism. Right totalitarianism draws its popular base principally from the middle class (which seeks to maintain the status quo and advance its own social position), whereas left totalitarianism relies primarily upon the lower class (which seeks egalitarianism). Moreover, right totalitarianism is outspokenly racist and elitist, whereas left totalitarianism is nonracist and, presumably, nonelitist. I say "presumably," because while right totalitarianism rests on the cult of the hero, left totalitarianism proclaims a belief in "collective leadership." In practice, however, the cults of Stalin and Mao have been as pronounced as those of Hitler and Mussolini.

A final difference lies in the role of terror and violence in the two types of totalitarian societies. Left totalitarianism comes to power through massive exercise of violence and terror and the elimination of all opponents—political, social, military, economic—in short order. Therefore, terror and violence tend to level off or actually decrease as left totalitarian regimes continue in power.* By contrast, rather than eliminating their opponents outright, right totalitarian regimes (particularly the Nazis) created a system of dual elites in which the old leaders continued to exist side by side (but were subordinated to) the new leaders. In other words, the old elites continued to pose as sources of threat and vulnerability. Accordingly, the level of terror and violence stayed constant or actually increased in those regimes. Right totalitarian regimes attempted to deflect attention from their vulnerability and insecurity by scapegoating the Jews or by undertaking expansive foreign policies or both. In so doing, they paved the way for their own eventual demise, whereas left totalitarian regimes have continued to flourish.

Having examined the totalitarianism of the Fascist and Nazi varieties, we turn to an examination of the Communist experience in the next three chapters. Before so doing, however, we should check the fit between these two ideologies and the analytical framework proposed in chapter one.

---

*Stalin's "Great Purge" of the 1930s constitutes a glaring exception, and it has been attributed to his pathological personality rather than to the needs of the Soviet system.

THE FRAMEWORK APPLIED

The cognitive dimension of fascism and nazism views the world in terms of a permanent struggle involving individuals, nations, and states. In such a world, will, power, strength, and force become indispensable for asserting oneself, one's nation, and one's state—and demonstrating superiority at all levels. Violence needs no other justification.

In some respects, the affective and evaluative components of fascism and nazism overlap to such an extent that it is difficult to separate them. Nationalism—the promised restoration of national greatness, pride, and honor—constitutes an irresistible value that is laden with equally irresistible emotional appeal. Racism—whether biological or cultural—has quite similar characteristics. In the 1920s and the 1930s, for example, it was apparently easy for many Germans to compensate for the humiliation of defeat by embracing the myth of Aryan supremacy and scapegoating the Jews.

Another aspect of the evaluative dimension is the glorification of the state—whether "corporate" or "folkish"—as the repository of all that is good and valuable. Similar attributes are associated with the party. And insofar as the superhuman leader-hero stands at the apex of both the party and the state—indeed, insofar as he personifies them—he assumes the highest value. Accordingly, total obedience and submission to the party/state/leader become values in themselves.

The programmatic component of fascism and nazism has two principal aspects. Internally, the party/state/leader launches a program of purifying the society of the "undesirable" elements and of improving the condition of the "desirable" ones. Externally, the party/state/leader embarks upon a policy of expansionism and imperialism in order to conquer other lands and acquire fresh "living space." The heroic deeds of the leader must find concrete expression at both the national and the international levels.

The social base of fascism and nazism is necessarily limited to the loyalists—to disciplined and slavish followers, to those of presumed cultural or racial purity, to the insecure members of the middle and lower classes. Fascism and nazism made systematic efforts to identify friends to be cultivated and enemies to be eliminated. Nothing came in between.

Selected Bibliography

Abel, Theodore. *The Nazi Movement.* New York: Atherton Press, 1965.

Arendt, Hannah. *The Origins of Totalitarianism.* New York: Harcourt, Brace, 1951.

Bracher, Karl D. *The German Dictatorship.* New York: Praeger, 1970.

Bullock, Alan. *Hitler: A Study in Tyranny.* New York: Harper & Row, 1964.

Cohen, Carl, ed. *Communism, Fascism, and Democracy.* 2nd ed. New York: Random House, 1972.

De Felice, Renzo. *Fascism: An Informal Introduction to Its Theory and Practice.* New Brunswick, N.J.: Transaction Books, 1976.

Erikson, Erik H. "The Legend of Hitler's Childhood." In *Childhood and Society.* 1950. Reprint. New York: Norton, 1963.

Fest, Joachim C. *Hitler.* New York: Random House, 1975.

Finer, Herman. *Mussolini's Italy.* London: Victor Gollanez, 1935.

Friedrich, Carl J., ed. *Totalitarianism.* Cambridge, Mass.: Harvard University Press, 1954.

Friedrich, Carl J., and Zbigniew Brzezinski. *Totalitarian Dictatorship and Autocracy.* 2nd ed. New York: Praeger, 1965.

Fromm, Erich. *Escape from Freedom.* New York: Holt, 1941.

Gregor, A. James. *Italian Fascism and Developmental Dictatorship.* Princeton: Princeton University Press, 1980.

———. *Young Mussolini and the Intellectual Origins of Fascism.* Berkeley: University of California Press, 1979.

Hitler, Adolf. *Mein Kampf.* Boston: Houghton Mifflin, 1962.

Langer, Walter C. *The Mind of Adolf Hitler.* New York: New American Library, 1978.

Merkl, Peter H. *The Making of a Stormtrooper.* Princeton: Princeton University Press, 1979.

———. *Political Violence under the Swastika.* Princeton: Princeton University Press, 1975.

Mosse, George L. *The Crisis of German Ideology: Intellectual Origins of the Third Reich.* New York: Grosset, 1964.

Mussolini, Benito. "The Doctrine of Fascism." Reprinted in *Communism, Fascism, and Democracy,* edited by Carl Cohen. 2nd ed. New York: Random House, 1972.

Neumann, Franz. *Behemoth: The Structure and Practice of National Socialism.* New York: Octagon Books, 1963.

Nolte, Ernst. *Three Faces of Fascism.* New York: New American Library, 1969.

Payne, Robert. *The Life and Death of Adolf Hitler.* New York: Popular Library, 1974.

Schapiro, Leonard. *Totalitarianism.* New York: Praeger, 1972.

Shirer, William L. *The Rise and Fall of the Third Reich.* New York: Touchstone Books, 1981.

Smith, Denis Mack. *Mussolini.* New York: Knopf, 1982.

Sorel, Georges. *Reflections on Violence.* 1906. Reprint. New York: Collier Books, 1961.

Speer, Albert. *Inside the Third Reich.* New York: Macmillan, 1981.

Toland, John. *Adolf Hitler.* New York: Ballantine Books, 1977.

Trevor-Roper, H. R. *The Last Days of Hitler.* New York: Macmillan, 1981.

Woolf, S. J., ed. *Fascism in Europe.* Rev. ed. New York: Methuen, 1982.

4

Marxism

As noted in chapter 1, the accelerating pace of urbanization and industrialization in the nineteenth century made for, among other things, the rapid rise of the proletariat, or industrial working class. In the person of Karl Marx (1818–1883), the proletariat found its *principal* analyst, philosopher, and ideologue.

Prior to Marx, needless to say, many "socialist thinkers" (as they are generically called) had written on the condition of the working class, most notably the Frenchman Charles Fourier (1772–1837), the Englishman Robert Owen (1771–1858), and the Swiss Jean Charles Sismondi (1773–1842). Karl Marx and his lifelong friend, collaborator, and benefactor Friedrich Engels (1820–1895), however, labeled all earlier thinkers "utopian" socialists, meaning that they were daydreamers and wishful thinkers dealing in imaginary situations. By contrast, Marx and Engels claimed to have founded "scientific" socialism by focusing on the hard facts of reality, namely the economic structure of societies and the social formations (that is, social classes) to which they give rise.

Marx's claim was only *that*, however, a claim unsubstantiated in his writings. In fact, as we shall see, Marx was a moralist from first to last. In a real sense, Marx's philosophy in all its ramifications amounts to a categorical denunciation of Western capitalist society as immoral, inhuman, and dehumanizing.

Since Marx wrote so prodigiously (nearly fifty volumes), we cannot possibly do justice to all aspects of his thinking. We can, however, cover the broad outlines of his intellectual concerns by focusing on a controversy that has raged in Marxist scholarship for a couple of decades. This controversy surrounds the periodization of Marx's writings and the issues of continuity or discontinuity that ensue therefrom.

Briefly, one group of scholars argues that the beginning of Marx's collaboration with Engels in 1845 marked a sharp departure from his earlier concerns. According to this group, there is a "Young," or "humanist," Marx and there is a "Mature," or "revolutionary," Marx, and the two are quite separate and distinct.

A second group of scholars stresses the continuity of Marx's thought, denying that the older Marx abandoned his youthful intellectual pursuits. According to this group, there is only one Marx, who undergoes a process of intellectual development, restating the same basic themes while using different modes of expression.

After we have examined the thought of Young Marx and of Mature Marx, we shall return to an evaluation of this controversy. First, however, it would be helpful to place Karl Marx in the context of the times in which he lived.

MARX AND HIS TIMES

Karl Marx was born in 1818 in the city of Trier (now in West Germany) to a moderately well-to-do family. His father, a lawyer by profession, was of Jewish origin but had converted to Protestantism, a religion Marx shared in his early youth.

At age seventeen, Marx went to study in Bonn and Berlin, finally receiving a doctorate in philosophy from the University of Jena in 1841 at age twenty-three. Having returned to Bonn in search of a teaching post, he found the doors closed because of both his Jewish name and a reputation he had developed as an atheist, radical, and subversive.

German universities at this time were hotbeds of intellectual and political activity, in which Marx had become totally immersed. Most of the intellectual ferment surrounded the ideas of the renowned philosopher G. W. F. Hegel (1770–1831), which drew both intense opposition and intense support.

Hegel's philosophy is too complicated to go into here. Suffice it to say, in *highly oversimplified* terms, that he was an idealist who (1) stressed the importance of spiritual and cultural forces and ideas in human history, (2) glorified the idea of the state as the embodiment of the highest spiritual force, which he called *Geist,* or Universal Spirit, and (3) generally defended and justified the status quo whether in religion, politics, or culture.

Marx devoted much time and effort in mastering Hegel's philosophical system, at the end only to transform and transcend it. As an intellectual "leftist" and "radical," he set out to set Hegel "right side up" or, alternatively, to "put him on his feet."

Meanwhile, in 1842, Marx turned to journalism, first as a writer for, and subsequently editor of, a major daily newspaper in Bonn. He used this post to expound his ideas on the freedom of the press, religion, and the like, and to write exposés on the conditions of poor and exploited people in the area (for example, the vineyard workers). As might be expected, Marx's journalism did not sit well with the authorities, who suppressed his newspaper in 1843.

Marx then emigrated to Paris, where he first met Friedrich Engels, a wealthy German industrialist who worked and lived in England. During his Paris years, Marx studied the works of English economists as well as of French and Russian socialists and anarchists. He also came into direct contact with the squalid conditions of urban workers, which further intensified his radicalism and found expression in his journalistic activities. In 1845, the Paris authorities, having decided that his contributions to a Franco-German journal were subversive, expelled him.

Marx moved to Brussels where there was a fairly large German émigré group, only to face yet another explusion within a few years. Meanwhile, he had come into contact with the leaders of the League of the Just, later renamed the Communist League, an organization heavily involved in the working-class movement. In order to provide the league with an ideological and philosophical perspective, Marx and Engels drafted the *Communist Manifesto* in 1848, calling for worldwide revolution to overthrow the ruling classes and bring about a new age of peace and brotherhood.

In 1849, Marx began his exile in London, where he lived the balance of his life. There, he gained fresh exposure to the wretched condition of the working classes and the oppression and exploitation under which they lived. This experience further documented and justified the depiction of the dismal lives of the English lower classes in Engels's *Condition of the Working Classes in England,* published in 1845.

Marx devoted the rest of his life to participating in radical activity, writing trenchant critiques of capitalism as an exploitative and inhuman economic system, and expounding the need for worldwide revolution. He did all this in the midst of either outright poverty or financial mismanagement. Three of Marx's children died for lack of food and medicine, and the whole family lived in a constant state of fear and anxiety.

Marx's wife, Jenny, to whom he was devoted from early youth, came from an aristocratic background, and in the 1870s, the family's financial situation improved, when she came into a substantial inheritance. The physical condition of both Marx and his wife soon began to deteriorate, however. Jenny's death in 1881 was a blow from which Marx never recovered. He died two years later, in 1883.

THE IDEAS OF MARX

Young Marx

The main source for the study of the thought of the Young Marx is the *Economic and Philosophical Manuscripts of 1844,* also known as the Paris Manuscripts (Paris being where Marx lived at the time). In this work Marx demonstrated a broad concern with human nature, human odyssey, and human destiny. The entire treatment, however, hinges on Marx's assumption of the primacy of human productive activity, in the course of which one comes to interact with oneself, with other human beings, and with nature.

Marx developed his argument with considerable philosophical subtlety. For our purposes, however, it may be simplified and summarized in terms of four central propositions.

Proposition 1: The human condition is a condition of labor, work, productivity, creativity.

Human beings, according to Marx, are by nature driven to productivity: they *must* work, they *must* produce. For Marx, labor is not merely a way of making a living; it is not the same as a job. Labor—*understood as productivity and creativity*—is the very essence of human personality. One expresses oneself in one's labor (whether intellectual or manual), one realizes oneself in one's labor—in a word, one lives one's life in one's labor. As such, labor, productivity, and creativity represent the epitome of human *fulfillment*. They are not to be seen as burden or drudgery.

Proposition 2: The condition of human labor (work, productivity, creativity) is that, ideally, it be voluntary and spontaneous.

In Proposition 1, Marx asserted, in effect, that labor is an expression of human personality. Proposition 2 simply modifies the first by asserting that labor should be a *voluntary* expression of human personality. Human beings, in other words, should have freedom to express themselves as they see fit and as they please. Accordingly, in a famous passage, Marx stated that, in the ideal society (that is, a society of economic abundance), one should have the opportunity to fish in the morning, hunt in the afternoon, and read plays in the evening, without having to be a professional fisherman or hunter or drama critic.

Proposition 3: The central problem of human life is that labor (work, productivity, creativity) has never been spontaneous or voluntary.

Throughout history, according to Marx, labor has involved compulsion and force. At every turn, the productive and creative personality has been exploited, oppressed, dispossessed, and brutalized. Throughout history, in short, human creativity has led to human *alienation*.

Alienation is a central theme of Young Marx and it deserves attention in some detail. Ordinarily understood as "separation" or "estrangement," Marx used the concept with considerable sophistication—and at several levels.

In the first place, Marx maintained, man is alienated from the *activity* of his own labor.* The reason is simply that forced labor is *against* human nature. In this sense human beings have been—quite literally—dehumanized. (Note Marx's assumption that, ideally, to be human is to labor voluntarily.)

Second, man has been alienated from the *products* of his own labor. The products of man's work—from the most mundane wares to the most imposing monuments—everywhere surround him but appear alien and hostile to him. The primary reason, again, is that man's productive activity is no longer voluntary self-activity. Man is no longer a creative being. Rather, he is forced to *sell* his labor for the production of commodities (as on the assembly line).

Third, man is alienated from other human beings who come together to form society. Forced labor, according to Marx, transforms society into a collection of alienated men and women—all production robots and automatons.

Finally, man is alienated from nature. Ideally, human beings interact with nature and use nature's resources—without, however, despoiling nature. Forced labor changes this condition as well: nature, too, is exploited and ravaged for someone else's advantage or profit.

On the whole, then, Marx concluded, there is a fundamental gap between *human essence* (voluntary productive activity) and *human existence* (forced and alienated labor).

Now, according to Marx, man in all societies is to some extent alienated. The peak of alienation, however, is reached in capitalist society, wherein man's labor results in the production of material objects (commodities) that (1) involve the most degrading forms of oppression and exploitation, and

---

*I use "man" generically and only for stylistic convenience. My meaning includes men and women—human beings of eitner gender.

(2) are exchanged for money. Capitalism, said Marx, is the "religion of money worship."

Proposition 4: The only solution to the problem of human life is revolution.

Man's experience of alienation can be broken only through a fundamental overturning of the social order. In Marx's terminology, "communist action" and "communist revolution" are designed as the means of eliminating alienation from man's experience, returning him to an ideal condition of voluntary and spontaneous productivity and creativity. At the end, in other words, man is restored to his original, and true, human nature: the unalienated producer and creator. In this sense, revolution is the supreme act of purification and creativity.

Such in brief is the thought of Young Marx. Although he postulated a human "essence" (in terms of productivity and creativity), it is clear that Marx saw man as a social product as well as a "species being." Human beings are thus flexible and malleable, changing from one society to another, one historical epoch to another. More precisely, insofar as man is a "productive being," he is a reflection of the economic system in which he finds himself. Hence, to change man, one must change the economic foundation of society.

Although perhaps beguiling and mesmerizing, the thought of Young Marx is laced with a series of difficulties. For one thing, there is his preemptive definition of "labor." Even under ideal conditions, can all labor be equally creative? Can human life be free of all drudgery? For another, there is Marx's rampant idealism. Even in ideal society, can human beings be uniformly good, selfless, and creative? Finally, there is Marx's failure to reconcile man's intrinsic need for spontaneous labor with the needs of the social order. If human beings are to do as they please, how then is social life possible?

Mature Marx

The thought of Mature Marx revolves around his materialist conception of history, also called dialectical materialism, which is Engels's phrase. In order to understand the materialist interpretation, one must first grasp Marx's view of society in general.

All human society, according to Marx, has two principal elements or components: a substructure and a superstructure. The substructure consists of material, economic forces that are *institutionalized*, or "externally" manifested, in social classes.* The chief determinant of class for Marx being ownership of the means of production (the assembly line is a prime example), he ends up with two classes: the owners, who are also the rulers and the exploiters, and the nonowners, who are also the ruled and the exploited. As is readily apparent, having come into being as a result of the division of labor (broadly speaking), the two classes are in a constant state of tension and conflict. The ruling class seeks to preserve its interests and maintain control through its coercive political arm, the state.

Material, economic forces, Marx insisted, are the most important, though not the only, forces in human society; moreover, they determine the shape of the superstructure. The superstructure consists of all other aspects or components of society: art, culture, religion, politics, ideas, and ideologies. The superstructure, in other words, is secondary and derivative, reflecting as it does the substructure upon which it rests, which in turn represents the interests of the ruling class.**

According to Marx's materialist interpretation, history has undergone distinct stages of development, of which the most important are, chronologically, the slave, the feudal, and the capitalist. The gens, or ancient tribal, society is actually the first stage, but we will skip it because its inclusion would complicate matters more than enlighten them.

Each stage of history is characterized by a distinct mode of production, a distinct set of classes, and conflict among those classes. Thus, the slave mode of production gives rise to two

---

*Economic forces constitute the "mode of production"; classes, the "social relations of production."

**It is in this context that Marx is said to have turned Hegel "right side up," since Hegel had stressed the primacy of spiritual, nonmaterial forces in the shaping of society.

classes, master and slave; the feudal mode of production, to lord and serf; the capitalist mode of production, to the bourgeoisie and the proletariat.

In each stage, Marx maintained, the dominant class brings into being a dominated class with which it is in simultaneous unity and opposition—unity, because without one class the other cannot exist (the two being interdependent); opposition, because the dominated class comes to resist oppression and exploitation. In each stage, oppression and exploitation eventually reach such intensity that, no longer tolerating the conditions in which it finds itself, the dominated class spontaneously rises to overthrow its masters.

In each phase of history, in other words, the primary means of social change is class struggle culminating in revolution. Accordingly, following the prefatory statement of the *Communist Manifesto,* we come upon the ringing statement: "The history of all hitherto existing society is the history of class struggles."

History, according to Marx, has its own locomotive, its own inner momentum. The last stage—capitalism—sees the most intense forms of oppression and exploitation, the inevitable rise of the proletariat, the overthrow of the bourgeoisie and its coercive political apparatus, the capitalist state. What is unique about the proletarian revolution, what distinguishes it from all previous revolutionary upheavals, is that it leads to the abolition of private ownership of the means of production—and hence of classes, class struggle, and the state. Following a short period of the "dictatorship of the proletariat," in which the attempts of the bourgeoisie to subvert the revolution and restore the status quo are thwarted, the transition to a "classless society" is completed. Humankind, we are told, reaches a utopia of harmony, peace, and plenty.

Such, in a simplified nutshell, is Mature Marx's materialist interpretation of history. Just as the thought of Young Marx is riddled with serious problems, so is that of Mature Marx. Are material forces, in fact, the most important in society? Is it not the case that intellectual, political, and spiritual forces frequently have a decisive bearing on the economic foundations of society?* Is class an exclusively economic phenomenon, to be understood simply in terms of ownership or nonownership? Are class conflict, violence, and revolution always progressive, as Marx assumes, leading human society to higher and higher stages of development? In what sense is Marx's analysis "scientific"?

One Marx

We are now in a position to return to the issue of the continuity or discontinuity of Marx's thought. From an *interpretive* point of view, we can see that certain themes run through *all* of Marx's writings: human suffering, human odyssey, human destiny. In effect, he uses two different sets of concepts or categories of thought to convey two different versions of the human odyssey. Focusing on the condition of the individual (as "species being"), Young Marx employed such ideas as labor, productivity, creativity, and alienation. Focusing on the condition of society, Mature Marx used such concepts as substructure, superstructure, division of labor, class, and class conflict. In each case, he expressed the moral outrage that he seemed to feel so intensely.

From an *evidential* standpoint, if we accept the year 1845 as the demarcation date between the "two" Marxes, as it is supposed to be, it would then logically follow that we would not expect to find any of the Young Marx's thoughts in his later works. This is not the case. In a major work, *The Grundrisse,* written in 1857 but not discovered until 1923 and not published in English until 1971, Marx set out to delineate the "first principles" or broad intellectual outlines of his future work. *The Grundrisse,* as it turns out, is a synthetic statement which contains as much about Marx's pre-1845 intellectual concerns as about his post-1845 ones. In short, as he grew intellectually, Marx underwent a process of "self-clarification" (to use his own terminology), deploying different modes

---

*In fairness to Marx, he did acknowledge this possibility, but only in passing and as a rare exception.

of expression to convey his preoccupations, as he deemed appropriate.

THE SIGNIFICANCE OF MARX

In this brief discussion of some aspects of the thought of Karl Marx, I have criticized him for a variety of shortcomings. If Marx is in fact so vulnerable on so many grounds, the question naturally arises as to why he is considered such an important figure in the history of Western thought, occupying as he does a most pivotal position.

First, Marx was a thinker on a grand scale, bringing together and synthesizing into a new mold a great deal of Western philosophy. In so doing, he gave an interpretation of human society for all time and all place. It is axiomatic that the more grandiose one's philosophizing, the more vulnerable one's position becomes.

Second, Marx offered a synthesis that is historically and dynamically based. As such, he was a philosopher of change, not of the status quo. In fact, according to Marx, the function of the philosopher is twofold: (1) to help explain change—that is, to be a thinker, and (2) to help bring about change—that is, to be an activist.

Third, Marx presented a dynamic historical analysis that is economically based, together with a thoroughgoing critique of capitalism.* Where Marx erred was in assuming, *on the whole,* the primacy of economic forces and in postulating a one-way relationship between economics and politics (as well as other aspects of society). The crucial lesson to be learned from Marx in this context is the *fusion* of politics and economics—their mutual interaction and reciprocal influence.

Fourth, Marx's central concern was not simply economic forces and conditions but the *human consequences* of economic activity. In this sense his detailed discussion of human alienation is remarkably acute and timely.

---

*In order to avoid repetition, further aspects of Marx's analysis of capitalism will be covered in the following chapter.

Fifth, although Marx's claim to science remains only a claim, it is important to realize that he *understood* what it takes to be a scientist. The problem is that his moral passion routinely drowned his scientific intention.

Finally, one must bear in mind Marx's contribution to the theory and practice of revolution. As modified, changed, adjusted, and applied to various social contexts by Lenin, Mao, and others, Marx's thought has literally changed the face of the earth. This, of course, is the subject of following chapters.

THE FRAMEWORK APPLIED

The cognitive dimension of Marxism sees the world as made up of potentially productive and creative human beings who are everywhere and at all times brutalized and dehumanized for the economic self-aggrandizement of a few. The primacy of economic forces and the institutionalization of ownership-as-the-arena-of-exploitation give rise to incessant class struggle, oppression, and alienation. Conflict, in other words, is inherent in the economic structure of society.

The overriding and unifying theme in Marxism, as we have seen, is moral outrage against the institutions and practices of Western capitalist societies. When combined with unceasing reminders of exploitation, brutalization, dehumanization, and alienation, this dimension provides one of the most potent emotional appeals in human history. Thus, to paraphrase, Marx's *Communist Manifesto* closes with the ringing exhortation: Workers of all countries unite. You have nothing to lose but your chains.

Ideally, the evaluative component of Marxism revolves around egalitarianism, communalism, and communal ownership and control of national wealth. All this is merely a step toward the realization of a classless society in some distant future—a society in which all conflict ends, peace and harmony prevail, human creativity finds complete fulfillment, and the formula "From each according to his ability, to each according to his need" is promulgated.

The programmatic ingredient of Marxism is weak and untenable in that it calls for spontaneous and successful risings of the oppressed against the oppressor. As we shall see, however, this weakness was amply remedied by Lenin and Mao, among others.

The social base of Marxism is, strictly speaking, fully internationalist: the proletariat, regardless of time and place. (In classless society, of course, *all* distinctions will presumably vanish into one harmonious human race.) In practice, however, as we shall see, Lenin and Mao turned Marxism into national enterprises. As a result, there is as much friction between Communist countries today as there is between any other groups.

Selected Bibliography

Avineri, Shlomo. *The Social and Political Thought of Karl Marx.* Cambridge: Cambridge University Press, 1970.

———, ed. *Marx's Socialism.* New York: Atherton Press, 1973.

Bober, M. M. *Karl Marx's Interpretation of History.* Rev. ed. New York: Norton, 1965.

Bottomore, T. B., ed. *Karl Marx: Early Writings.* London: C. A. Watts, 1963.

Cohen, G. A. *Karl Marx's Theory of History: A Defense.* Princeton: Princeton University Press, 1979.

Fromm, Erich. *Marx's Concept of Man.* New York: Frederick Ungar, 1961.

Gilbert, Alan. *Marx's Politics: Communists and Citizens.* New Brunswick, N.J.: Rutgers University Press, 1981.

Heilbroner, Robert L. *Marxism: For and Against.* New York: Norton, 1980.

Koren, Henry J. *Marx and the Authentic Man.* New York: Humanities Press, 1973.

Marx, Karl. *Collected Works* or *Selected Works,* various editions.

———. *The Grundrisse.* 1857. Edited and translated by David McLellan. New York: Harper & Row, 1971.

McLellan, David. *Karl Marx: His Life and Thought.* New York: Harper & Row, 1974.

McMurtry, John. *The Structure of Marx's World-View.* Princeton: Princeton University Press, 1978.

Meszaros, Istvan. *Marx's Theory of Alienation*. London: Merlin Press, 1970.

Ollman, Bertell. *Alienation: Marx's Conception of Man in Capitalist Society*. 2nd ed. Cambridge: Cambridge University Press, 1976.

Tucker, Robert C. *The Marxian Revolutionary Idea*. New York: Norton, 1969.

———. *Philosophy and Myth in Karl Marx*. Cambridge: Cambridge University Press, 1961.

5

Leninism

As Marx matured intellectually, he became increasingly interested in the analysis and critique of the capitalist economic system and in the projection of its early demise due to the many problems that beset it. Specifically, he called for "proletarian revolutions" in the most advanced capitalist countries, where the proletariat is numerous—namely, Britain, France, Germany, and the United States. Marx expected these revolutions eventually to spread to engulf the entire globe.

Several decades after Marx's projections, the first "proletarian revolution" did occur—not in an advanced capitalist country but in backward Russia! How does one "explain" this momentous, yet unanticipated event?

The burden of "explanation"—and much more—falls primarily on the shoulders of one Vladimir Ilyich Ulyanov, better know as Lenin (1870–1924). Repeatedly invoking Marx's own dictum that "theory is a guide to action," Lenin set out to give the world a historic lesson: rather than studying Marxism "in the abstract," one can shape, bend, and apply it to the concrete conditions of specific countries. Given great determination and skill—and a large measure of luck—one might just succeed!

In the pages that follow, I shall discuss some of the major changes Lenin introduced in Marx's thought and then assess the significance of these changes for Marx's original formulations. What, I will be asking in effect, is left of Karl Marx once Lenin gets done with him? What contributions, if any, does Lenin make to the theory and practice of revolution? What does it all add up to?

Before proceeding, let us place Lenin in the context of his times.

LENIN AND HIS TIMES

Lenin was born in the provincial town of Simbirsk, on the Volga, to an educated middle-class family. His father was a secondary school teacher who, after years of service, was appointed czarist school administrator for the province of Simbirsk, a position that carried a minor nobility title.

Lenin's childhood and early youth were "normal" by conventional standards. A good student, athlete, and chess player, he gave no sign of becoming a revolutionary. He was an avid reader, at home with Russian literary and political writings. Through his father, however, he became familiar with the grim condition of the peasants and the arbitrariness with which government officials treated them.

Lenin's tranquil youth was jolted by the death of his father in 1886. A second trauma was the arrest and execution, in 1887, of his older brother Alexander for plotting to assassinate the czar. This event, Lenin claimed, set him on a revolutionary course.

Admitted to the University of Kazan (near which the family had moved), Lenin was later arrested and expelled for participation in student protest activity. Determined to pursue his studies, however, he plunged into a program of intense independent work, took a series of "external examinations," and obtained a law degree from the University of St. Petersburg in 1891.

A lawyer, however, Lenin was never to be. By this time, he had become well steeped in Marxist and anarchist literature and had come into contact with a variety of radical groups in Kazan, St. Petersburg, and elsewhere.

Lenin was arrested in 1895 for conspiring to publish an illegal newspaper and exiled to Siberia, where he was kept until 1900. During this period, he devoted much time to the analysis of the situation in Russia and the strategy and tactics of engineering a successful revolution against the czar. His principal conclusion was that nothing could be accomplished until a well-disciplined Communist party was organized and prepared for action.

Forbidden to participate in political activity in Russia, Lenin went into exile in Switzerland in 1900, where he sought to organize such a party and draft a revolutionary program. After reentering Russia in 1905 for a few months of clandestine activity, he returned to exile in Finland, Switzerland, and other European countries, where he remained until 1917.

Lenin's years of exile were characterized by unceasing efforts, through friends, supporters, and intermediaries, to incite radical activity in major Russian cities, eliminate opposition parties and groups, and eventually topple the czar. As a result, even while in exile he became the best known of the many Russian revolutionaries.

Lenin paid particular attention to the activities of the Russian Social Democratic Workers' party. As early as 1903, the party had broken into two wings: the Bolsheviks (the majority) and the Mensheviks (the minority). In 1912, the Bolshevik faction organized itself into a separate party under Lenin's leadership.

Its political ineptitude and financial bankruptcy having been exacerbated by the strains of World War I, the czarist regime collapsed in February 1917, to be replaced by a provisional government, which included Alexander Kerensky, a Social Democrat, who became premier in July. Having determined to return to Russia, Lenin and other Russian political émigrés obtained permission to travel through Germany and other countries in a sealed railway car, reaching the Finland Station in Petrograd in April. Following months of ceaseless agitation, Lenin led the Bolsheviks in the power seizure of October 1917. A period of illness ended in his death in 1924.

THE IDEAS OF LENIN

Concept of Imperialism

First, let us discuss Lenin's concept of imperialism and then examine some of its significant ramifications. I will draw heavily on Lenin's 1916 pamphlet, *Imperialism: The Highest Stage of Capitalism.*

Lenin's primary purpose in writing this pamphlet was to provide an explanation of why, contrary to Marx's expectations, capitalism had not collapsed. A related purpose was to reiterate and refine a thesis he had first developed in 1905 concerning the possibilities of proletarian revolutions in underdeveloped countries.

Lenin accepted Marx's analysis of capitalism as an economy of perpetual crises and proceeded to project the analysis to the global level. His central argument was that, unforeseen by Marx, capitalism had undergone a fundamental transformation by becoming international in scope. In other words, national (or domestic) capitalism had not collapsed because it had broadened its horizons by becoming international—that is to say, imperialist—in nature. Accordingly, for Lenin the shortest possible definition of imperialism was "international capitalism."

The capitalist economy, Lenin agreed with Marx, is an economy racked by chronic crises, particularly those of overproduction, underconsumption, and monopoly formation. Overproduction, Lenin argued, is due to capitalist greed and the concomitant attempt to maximize profits. Underconsumption, on the other hand, arises from the increasing inability of the lower and middle classes (presumably because of increasing oppression and exploitation) to afford capitalist goods and products. The combined net result, according to Lenin, is the saturation of the domestic market: it can absorb no more goods and commodities.

Meanwhile, monopoly formation has moved apace in the areas of both industry and finance.* As for industrial monopo-

---

*Monopoly formation suggests, by the way, that capitalism is destructive of its own essence: competition. This in turn echoes Marx's description of capitalists as "their own gravediggers."

lies, Lenin insisted, the time will come when, having wiped out all smaller and medium-sized enterprises, a handful of gigantic industrial concerns will control the economic life of the country.

The formation of industrial monopolies goes hand in hand with the emergence of banking and financial monopolies. This is because credit is central to capitalist economic life. The ability to buy, expand, innovate, and the like all depend on the availability of credit. And credit, of course, is controlled by banking and financial institutions.

In short, then, through the monopoly and manipulation of credit, financial institutions come to hold the power of life and death over industrial institutions. The result is the union of industrial and financial institutions—"finance capital," in Lenin's words—and the saturation of the domestic market not only of goods and commodities but of investment potential as well. To paraphrase, it simply does not "pay" to invest in the domestic market for *any* purpose.

What is the net outcome of all this? Will capitalism come to a standstill? Will it end?

Of course not, said Lenin. Having exhausted the domestic market, capitalism turns outward—to international markets. In fact, it begins a search not only for overseas markets, but also for overseas sources of investment, raw materials, and cheap labor. Such is the process of internationalization—or externalization—of capitalism.

Two important points need clarification before we look at the consequences of this internationalization. First, I have been talking as if a single capitalist country is undergoing this transformation. In fact, however, any number of capitalist states (some more advanced than others, to be sure) are experiencing similar developments.

Second, critical in the process of internationalization of capitalism is the role of the capitalist state. (State, it will be recalled, is the coercive political agent of the dominant class.) The capitalist search for overseas markets and the rest is undertaken by the capitalist state, using the most effective and convenient means: colonization. So begins, Lenin argued, the feverish hunt by capitalist countries for colonies or "unoccupied territories."

The capitalist hunt for colonies, according to Lenin, is bound to lead to a series of wars and conflicts as a result of which capitalism will finally collapse. To begin with, Lenin maintained, there will be wars between capitalist states and the peoples of the colonies. At some point in time, having attained political consciousness, the colonial peoples will rise in armed struggles to overthrow their foreign oppressors. In these struggles, moreover, the socialist countries, whose emergence Lenin saw over the horizon, as it were, will firmly side with the peoples of the colonies.

Beyond this, said Lenin, there will be wars *among* the capitalist powers themselves because as time goes on there will be less and less to colonize—all "unoccupied territories" will eventually be occupied. Since, being greedy, capitalist countries seek to dominate rather than cooperate, the only remaining alternative is to fight each other for control of the same colonies.

These conflicts and wars, Lenin concluded, spell the end of capitalism. Capitalism, he maintained, is doomed to fail—it is only temporarily and superficially strong. As such, capitalism is a "colossus with feet of clay."

Lenin's concept of imperialism, though containing an obvious grain of truth, is afflicted by some serious weaknesses. For instance, his discussion of capitalist overproduction and underconsumption overlooks the principle of supply and demand. It also overlooks the fact that, generally speaking, the twentieth century has seen an improvement (rather than a deterioration) in the condition of the working classes in capitalist societies, so that they *can* afford the goods and commodities the capitalist economy turns out.

Similarly, Lenin's discussion of monopoly formation ignores the emergence of antitrust laws, regulatory commissions, and government control of the economy.* Generally, Lenin's critique is more appropriate for "pure" capitalism (if such a thing ever existed) than for modern regulated capitalism.

Finally, the kinds of conflicts and wars Lenin projects have

---

*In the United States, for example, the Interstate Commerce Commission was formed as early as 1887.

either not materialized or, if they have (as in the two world wars), capitalism has been able to weather them.

The significance of Lenin's concept of imperialism is two-fold. First, it extends Marx's critique of capitalism by giving a fairly "reasonable" explanation (at least superficially and partially) of why capitalism has not collapsed. This hardly requires further elaboration.

Second, Lenin's concept of imperialism extends Marx's conception of revolution by allowing for the occurrence of proletarian revolutionary movements in underdeveloped—that is, nonproletarian—countries. Here imperialism becomes, in effect, the instigating and the precipitating force.

Concept of Revolution

Communist revolutions in advanced countries, Lenin maintained, will be accompanied by revolutionary movements in underdeveloped or colonial lands because capitalism is now a global, rather than a national, phenomenon, and the colonies are its inseparable extensions. Lenin developed an analogy likening imperialism to a global chain having many links; and he argued that a revolution will occur in *any* country—advanced or colonial—that happens to be the "weakest link" in this chain of capitalism. In a word, according to Lenin, there are two types of Communist revolutions: those occurring in advanced capitalist countries and those occurring in undeveloped colonial lands.

Communist revolutions in advanced countries follow Marx's model: having reached sufficient consciousness, the proletariat presumably engineers a revolution and overthrows the bourgeoisie. Communist revolutions in underdeveloped countries follow a different path, going through two stages of development.

The first stage, labeled "bourgeois-democratic," sees the alliance of the proletariat (under the leadership of the Communist party) with all social forces, classes, and groups that for whatever reason oppose feudalism, czarism, or imperialism, as the case may be. In other words, the proletariat, being small, cannot engineer a revolution on its own strength alone. It must form "united fronts" with all social strata that, inspired by nationalist and democratic sentiments, oppose the status quo. Of primary importance in this regard are the middle-class nationalists (businessmen, merchants, shopkeepers, civil servants, intellectuals); of secondary importance, the peasantry. Although the middle class and the peasantry do not want a Communist revolution, they share certain interests with the Communists in their distaste for oppression and exploitation. Hence, they can be used and manipulated. With Lenin, the exploitation of the nationalist sentiment in the service of communism becomes a hallmark of Communist theory and practice.

Having engineered a "bourgeois-democratic" revolution and having consolidated sufficient power, the proletariat now turns on its former allies, persecutes and eliminates them (as necessary) and pushes the revolution to its second stage, the "proletarian-socialist"—better known as a Communist takeover. Hence, in Russia, for example, the Communists (Bolsheviks) formed an alliance with the Nationalists (Mensheviks), Social Democrats, liberals, and other "progressive" forces to overthrow czarism and feudalism in February 1917. In October of that year, they took over in an outright power seizure.

It is clear that Lenin's "two-stage" notion of revolution, as it is called, is a far cry from Marx's conception of a proletarian revolution. Rather, it is a "pragmatic" or opportunistic adaptation of Marxist doctrine subsequently imitated and applied by revolutionary leaders in many parts of the world.

The genesis of the two-stage concept is to be found in the abortive February Revolution of 1905. On that "Bloody Sunday," after years of labor unrest, riots, and strikes (to which the czarist regime responded only with empty promises), the urban masses stormed the czar's palace (and other strategic centers) in St. Petersburg. Commanding overwhelming firepower, the czar's forces made short work of the uprising, killing hundreds (by some accounts, thousands) of people in the process.

Having begun as a textbook case of Marx's spontaneous revolution, the February event had a crucial impact on

Lenin's thinking. Specifically, ever sensitive to developments in Russia, Lenin drew two principal conclusions. First, he thought, the Russian proletariat was too small and too weak to attempt a revolution on its own strength alone—hence, the necessity for alliances with all other social forces in a two-stage revolutionary movement. Second, Lenin asserted, having been manifestly demonstrated wrong, Marx's notion of revolutionary spontaneity had to be replaced by something far more concrete, something that had preoccupied Lenin for some years.

Concepts of Party and State

Rejecting Marx's idea of spontaneity outright, Lenin insisted that the proletarian revolution requires leadership, organization, planning, and hard work. The principal agent for engineering and pushing the revolution forward must be the Communist party.

Lenin's concept of the party was fashioned in *What Is to Be Done?*, a pamphlet written in 1902, and it remains the foundation of all Communist party-building up to this day. The revolutionary party, Lenin insisted, must be an elitist organization: small, tightly knit, highly disciplined, and secret in character. At least in its initial stages, revolutionary struggle cannot be entrusted to everyone. In order to move ahead with the tasks of organization, mobilization, and consolidation, revolutionary activity must be in the hands of those with talent, skill, and dedication. In a word, to use his famous description, Lenin called for an organization of "professional revolutionaries"—that is to say, of those who have devoted their entire lives to revolution, who have turned revolution into a calling and a vocation.

Consisting as it does of the best-qualified revolutionaries, the party, according to Lenin, is the "vanguard"* of the proletariat in every sense. It is the only instrument capable of bringing political consciousness to the proletariat. (On its

---

*Or "advance guard"—the military connotation is quite intentional.

own, Lenin believed, the proletariat could develop only "trade-union consciousness.") It is the only instrument capable of organizing and mobilizing the proletariat. It is the only instrument capable of leading the proletariat in political struggle and armed struggle, legal struggle and illegal struggle.

It is obvious, then, that although elitist in nature, the Communist party cannot separate itself from the masses. On the contrary, the party must go among the masses, appeal to their self-interest and emotions, persuade them to identify the party's interest as their own, rally them to the cause, draw them into revolutionary action, deploy and coordinate their energies toward the realization of revolutionary objectives.

If it is to accomplish its goals, the party must have cohesion, solidarity, discipline, control, and, above all, unquestioned command and leadership. Factionalism and dissent cannot be permitted or tolerated. The party, in other words, is a monolithic organization. Nonetheless, since minority views and challenges to leadership are likely to emerge from time to time, the party must periodically purge itself of all "opportunist" and "deviationist" elements. No challenges to party leadership can be allowed.

At the societal level, the Leninist principle governing party organization is "democratic centralism." The centralism of this concept means that the party is a rigid hierarchy extending from the national to the regional, provincial, and municipal levels. At the lowest level are "primary party organizations," better known as Communist cells: in every office, every shop, every factory, party agents, however few, must always be on guard, protecting party interests and providing appropriate indoctrination. At the national level, all decision making is in the hands of a few men, most importantly the top leader (Lenin, Stalin . . . Andropov). The lines of authority (running downward) and of responsibility (running upward) are inflexible and absolute. Every higher level has absolute authority over every lower level; every lower level is absolutely responsible to every higher level.

The "democracy" part of democratic centralism suggests that at *each* level, party members have an opportunity to engage in discussion and debate before decisions are made. In effect, however, all decisions for any one level are made by party leaders at the immediately higher level. "Democracy," then, is simply a means of creating the illusion of participation and decision making, thereby keeping party members pacified, if not contented.

In any event, the most important objective of the Communist party for the immediate future is to plan, engineer, and execute the overthrow of the capitalist state. Having done this, it will establish a transitional political apparatus—the "dictatorship of the proletariat"—in order to eliminate all opposition and thwart any potential attempt at restoration of the old regime.

So far, Lenin's notion of the state is identical to that of Marx. Lenin departed from Marx, however, in arguing that the state as a political apparatus will continue to exist after the dictatorship of the proletariat has been completed. Specifically, he distinguished between "socialism" and "communism" (classless society), insisting that the state will disappear in the Communist (not the socialist) stage.

The "socialist state" must exist in order to perform two important functions. First, said Lenin, the exploiting classes can be wiped out only gradually and not overnight—and as long as there are classes, there will be a state. Second, "socialism" is the first necessary step toward the construction of a Communist society of abundance governed by the formula, "From each according to his work, to each according to his need." This task, too, requires the political power of the state.*

THE SIGNIFICANCE OF LENIN

Lenin, it is by now clear, made a series of concrete changes in Marxist doctrine. He modified Marx's interpretation of history by adding a substage that he called imperialism. He

---

*Subsequent Communist thinkers have abandoned altogether Marx's idea of the disappearance of the state. In fact, in all Communist countries today, the state plays the preeminent role in all societal spheres.

changed Marx's conception of revolution to account for proletarian upheavals in both advanced and developing countries. He rejected Marx's idea of spontaneity by insisting on leadership, organization, and mobilization. He modified Marx's concept of the state by stipulating the continuing necessity for a "socialist" political apparatus. These changes, by the way, can be viewed either as an abandonment of Marx, as some maintain, or as a development of Marx, as others argue.

In any event, these changes are important enough in and of themselves. They are so important, in fact, that henceforth they turned "Marxism" into "Marxism-Leninism." Nonetheless, these specific changes do not address the overall significance of Lenin.

The overall significance of Lenin is to be found in two areas. First, whereas Marx had stressed the fusion of economics and politics while assigning primacy to economic forces, Lenin reversed the relationship by assigning primacy to the political sphere. Economic analysis was important to Lenin, to be sure, as seen in his concept of imperialism. But far more important were such political considerations as class alliance and united front, leadership and organization (chiefly the party), socialist state, and socialist construction.

Second, Lenin *demonstrated* once and for all that Marxist ideology, far from being just another set of mental abstractions, can be put to work to overturn political regimes and change the lives of millions. Herein lies the "magic" of Lenin; and in the long run this becomes more important than any specific change or contribution he introduced.

THE FRAMEWORK APPLIED

The cognitive dimension of Leninism views the world as consisting of a relatively few people of wealth, privilege, and status on the one hand, and the masses of exploited workers on the other. Class warfare is inevitable and persistent until such time as the whole social system is overturned.

The affective component of Leninism appeals to all oppressed classes to unite in a common struggle for justice and revenge. The evaluative ingredient promises, literally, a new world in which all wrongs have been righted. The affective *and* evaluative dimensions of Leninism are potently captured in the following lines from *L'Internationale,* the official song of the Communist International (Comintern), established by Lenin in 1919:

> Arise you prisoners of starvation,
> Arise you wretched of the earth,
> For justice thunders condemnation,
> A better world's in birth.
> No more tradition's chains shall bind us,
> Arise you slaves, no more in thrall,
> The earth shall rise on new foundations,
> We have been naught, we shall be all.

The programmatic component of Leninism rests on a two-stage urban revolutionary strategy stressing the indispensability of leadership, organization, and class alliance (particularly with middle-of-the-road nationalists). Only through hard work can the masses be mobilized. Only through mobilization can a revolutionary movement gain momentum.

In theory the social base of Leninism is internationalist. In practice, however, Lenin turned Marxism into a national phenomenon resting primarily on the working class and secondarily on the peasantry, leadership always coming from the middle-class intellectuals, who form the core of the Communist party. At some unspecified moment in the future, however, Lenin expected communism to become an international reality.

Selected Bibliography

Bunyon, James, and H. H. Fisher. *The Bolshevik Revolution, 1917–1918.* Stanford: Stanford University Press, 1934.

Carr, Edward Hallett. *The Bolshevik Revolution, 1917–1923.* Vol. 1. New York: Macmillan, 1951.

Chamberlin, William Henry. *The Russian Revolution, 1917–1921.* 2 vols. New York: Macmillan, 1935.

Conquest, Robert. *V. I. Lenin.* New York: Viking, 1972.

Deutscher, Isaac. *Lenin's Childhood.* New York: Oxford University Press, 1970.

Fischer, Louis. *The Life of Lenin.* New York: Harper & Row, 1964.

Hill, Christopher. *Lenin and the Russian Revolution.* New York: Macmillan, 1950.

Lenin, V. I. *Collected Works* or *Selected Works,* various editions.

Meyer, Alfred G. *Leninism.* New York: Praeger, 1962.

Payne, Robert. *The Life and Death of Lenin.* New York: Simon & Schuster, 1964.

Shub, David. *Lenin.* New York: Doubleday, 1948.

Theen, Rolf H. W. *Lenin: Genesis and Development of a Revolutionary.* Philadelphia: Lippincott, 1973.

Trotsky, Leon. *The History of the Russian Revolution.* 1 vol. ed. New York: Simon & Schuster, 1936.

———. *Lenin: Notes for a Biographer.* New York: Putnam, 1971.

———. *The Young Lenin.* New York: Doubleday, 1972.

Ulam, Adam B. *The Bolsheviks: The Intellectual and Political History of the Triumph of Communism in Russia.* New York: Macmillan, 1965.

Wilson, Edmund. *To the Finland Station.* New York: Doubleday, 1940.

Wolfe, Bertram D. *Three Who Made a Revolution.* Rev. ed. New York: Dial Press, 1964.

Wolfenstein, E. Victor. *The Revolutionary Personality: Lenin, Trotsky, Gandhi.* Princeton: Princeton University Press, 1967.

① Read Goodwin,
    Chaps. 1 & 2

② Read Rajai, ~~Chaps.~~
        all

③ Go Back and read
    the rest of goodwin.

④ Come back!

Norman Cohen,
    The Pursuit of
the Milennium -

Operator _____

_____

_____

_____

_____

_____

Message _____

RETURNED YOUR CALL	

TELEPHONED		PLEASE CALL	
CALLED TO SEE YOU		WILL CALL AGAIN	
WANTS TO SEE YOU		URGENT	

Phone _____

Area Code	Number	Extension

of _____

M _____

WHILE YOU WERE OUT

To _____

Date 7/25   Time 9:40

6
Maoism

Marx fashioned a theory of revolution appropriate, he thought, for advanced capitalist societies. Invoking Marx's dictum that "theory is a guide to action," Lenin modified, adjusted, bent, and applied Marx's theory to czarist, semifeudal-semicapitalist Russia. Accepting Lenin's changes and modifications, Mao Tse-tung* (1893–1976) proceeded to give Marxism-Leninism a "Chinese" flavor—that is to say, make it applicable to the specific conditions of China. Marxism, he insisted, must be given "a definite national form" before it can be put into practice.

What does Mao's "national form" consist of? What are the principal features of Chinese communism as conceived and practiced by Mao Tse-tung?

At the risk of simplification, I suggest that the most important features of Mao Tse-tung's thought are to be found in three areas:

1. the shift of the locus of revolution from the urban centers to the countryside
2. the formation of a long-term alliance with the peasantry, as well as with other social classes

---

*I use the Wade-Giles system of romanizing Chinese names in order to maintain consistency with the bibliographical entries, all of which were published before the new system went into effect.

3. the development of a protracted revolutionary struggle beginning with peasant guerrilla warfare and culminating in full-scale conventional military confrontations.

Also notable is the attempt to project on the global level the entire revolutionary strategy of Mao Tse-tung.

Let us begin by taking a brief look at Mao's life and times.

MAO AND HIS TIMES

Mao Tse-tung was born in 1893 in the village of Shao Shan, Hunan province, a traditional hotbed of radical activity. Mao's father had gradually risen from the status of a poor peasant to that of a rich peasant, which meant he owned land and was a grain merchant.

Mao's father was a tyrant who ran his business with a firm hand, maltreating, humiliating, and punishing anyone who disobeyed him. His harshness did not spare even Mao, who came to resent his father and rebelled against him. As a result, Mao's childhood was highlighted by a long series of family conflicts. Simultaneously, he observed in microcosm and at firsthand the plight of the Chinese peasant.

Mao's formal schooling was minimal, but he was a voracious reader throughout his life and did a great deal of independent study. He read widely in Eastern as well as in Western literature and philosophy.

Mao lived in Peking in 1918–1919 and held a minor post at Peking University library under Li Ta-chao, a leading Marxist intellectual. In this capacity, Mao met a variety of other radical intellectuals and read extensively in Marxist literature. By the summer of 1920, Mao considered himself a Marxist.

Mao's radicalization must be seen in the context of Chinese history in the first few decades of the twentieth century. Briefly, these decades were ones of intense intellectual and political ferment, centering primarily on two groups, the Nationalists and the Communists.

The key figure in the Nationalist movement was Sun Yat-sen (1867–1925). Educated in Hong Kong and Hawaii, converted to Christianity at age eighteen, impatient with Chinese traditions, Sun sought to create a new China representing a fusion of Oriental and Western values—a China free of foreign rule, politically strong, and economically prosperous. His objectives were spelled out in the Three People's Principles: nationalism, democracy, and people's welfare.

The accidental explosion of a bomb in a warehouse in Hankow in October 1911 ignited a popular uprising that spread rapidly across many provinces and eventually marked the overthrow of the hated Manchu regime. Sun Yat-sen was inaugurated as provisional president of the Republic on January 1, 1912.

Throughout his life, Sun sought to unify China and create a viable national government. To these ends, he welcomed cooperation with the Communists, with whom he formed an alliance in 1924. Sun's efforts were ended by his death in 1925. Taking Sun's place was Chiang Kai-shek (1887–1975), an ultraconservative who was deeply hostile toward the Communists.

The formal beginning of the Communist movement in China may be dated with the founding of the Chinese Communist party (CCP) in 1921. By this time communism had become a familiar ideology to many Chinese intellectuals and many Communist study groups had been established in the major cities. Having represented his home province at the founding of the CCP, Mao returned to Hunan to assume the post of provincial party secretary.

In April 1927, Chiang Kai-shek staged a massive night coup in Shanghai, killing thousands of Communists and labor leaders, eliminating the labor movement in that city, and virtually destroying the proletarian base of the CCP. Although the experience was disastrous for the Communists, they learned the importance of military strength and their vulnerability to enemy attacks in the major cities.

In September 1927, Mao Tse-tung organized a peasant uprising to coincide with the autumn harvest in Hunan. The uprising failed, and he led a contingent of armed peasants into the rugged mountains of Kiangsi. There he created a revolutionary base, set up a worker-peasant government, and launched a program of land reform. For the next three years, in relative isolation from government troops, Mao and his associates concentrated on building their military forces and expanding their "liberated areas."

In 1934, Chiang Kai-shek launched the last of a series of five campaigns (the first four having failed) to wipe out the Communists and destroy their strongholds. Employing overwhelming military power and a policy of multiple blockades, he was able to overpower the Communist forces. The Communists faced the alternatives of either being completely destroyed or trying to crash through Chiang's lines. Thus they began, on October 15, 1934, the famous Long March from Kiangsi (southeast China) to Shensi (north-central China). Taking a year to complete, this epic adventure covered some six thousand miles of deserts, mountains, and rivers.

Committing military blunders and following a predictable course, the Communists suffered heavy casualties. Because of the severity of the situation, the top leadership group held a meeting in January 1935. Having consolidated power, Mao emerged as undisputed leader—a position he was to hold for about three decades.

When the Japanese launched a full-scale invasion of China in 1937, the Communists immediately stressed national unity and resistance to the outsider as taking precedence over all other tasks. Their continued appeal to Chinese nationalism vastly enhanced their popularity in northern China. And they capitalized on the enormous prestige of Sun Yat-sen by formally adopting his Three People's Principles as their "minimum program."

When the Japanese surrendered in August 1945, the Communists were fully prepared to turn the anti-Japanese war into a "people's war" against Chiang Kai-shek and his corrupt government. The balance of forces between the two sides rapidly changed in favor of the Communists. From 1947 on, Chiang's troops suffered consistent defeats at the hands of Mao's People's Liberation Army. Rapidly withdrawing from the major cities, Chiang Kai-shek finally retreated to Taiwan. Mao Tse-tung proclaimed the Chinese People's Republic on October 1, 1949. He remained the key charismatic figure throughout the turbulence of Chinese politics of the ensuing decades until his death in 1976.

THE IDEAS OF MAO

The Locus of Revolution

Up until the time of Mao Tse-tung, revolutionary leaders (Communist and non-Communist alike) had considered the urban centers as the principal locations of revolutionary activity. They had uniformly stressed coordinated insurrections in the major cities, capturing the regime's key power centers and paralyzing the government literally in its "seat." In contrast to all this, Mao proposed to relocate the center of revolution to the countryside as the *necessary* first step toward eventual power seizure. The resultant "rural" revolutionary strategy is rooted in Mao's extensive analyses of the conditions of Chinese society and how best to apply Marxism-Leninism to that particular set of circumstances.

To begin with, Mao identified China as a semifeudal and semicolonial country. A semifeudal society is one in which elements of feudalism exist side by side with elements of capitalism. In such a country, there is a small but powerful big bourgeoisie (upper and upper-middle classes), just as there is a small but powerful landlord class. There is also a small and weak proletariat, a small middle (or national) bourgeoisie, a medium-sized lower (or petty) bourgeoisie, and above all, vast masses of peasants. The coexistence of a multiplicity of social forces suggests that the revolutionaries must develop the foresight and skill to exploit existing grievances and injustices and to form alliances with any social group that for whatever reason may support them.

A semicolonial country, according to Mao, is one under the simultaneous influence of several imperialist powers. In China, these powers included Britain, France, Germany, Japan, and the United States. Not only are competition and conflict bound to develop among the several imperialist countries, these frictions are also bound to be reflected in the reactionary domestic groups that support them because they benefit from their presence. Hence the revolutionaries must become especially alert to exploiting all conflicts and rivalries to their own advantage. Moreover, given the sheer presence of the outsiders, the revolutionaries must do all they can to appeal to nationalist sentiments and emotions. Accordingly, Mao paid far more attention to fusing communism and nationalism than any revolutionary before him. And in so doing, he established a pattern for many colonial revolutions of the postwar era.

A semifeudal and semicolonial country is, by definition, a partially developed country. This means, in practical terms, that the power of imperialist, governmental, and other "reactionary" forces is concentrated in a relatively few urban and industrial centers while the great expanses of the country remain beyond their interest, control, or both.

Hence, Mao concluded, being initially weak, the revolutionaries cannot take on the enemy in his strongholds and on his own terms. Rather, if they are to succeed, revolutionary forces must retreat to inaccessible rural areas, wait out their time, mobilize and consolidate their strength gradually, and then surround the cities and strangle them.

This was a whole new strategy of revolution, successfully employed in China beginning in the late 1920s and culminating in the seizure of power in 1949.

Mao's rural strategy confronted vigorous opposition from the Soviet Union, which, under Stalin, erroneously sought to impose the "Soviet model" on China. Mao also faced serious resistance within the Chinese Communist party, whose early leadership was dominated by pro-Soviet elements. By the mid-1930s, however, Mao Tse-tung was able to consolidate his position within the party, reject the Soviet line, and emerge as the undisputed leader.

The Peasantry as a Revolutionary Force

One of the chief characteristics of an unevenly developed country, as we have seen, is the presence of a large peasant population. Having come from a peasant background himself, Mao Tse-tung paid particular attention to the Chinese peasantry and their revolutionary potential.

Since Marx's focus was advanced capitalist countries, he paid relatively little attention to the peasants as a revolutionary force. Lenin did stress the importance of the peasantry, but only in the first stage of the revolution, the "bourgeois democratic"; beyond that, he was contemptuous and distrustful of the peasants. By contrast, Mao's faith in the peasantry was total and unqualified: they remained allies from first to last.

As early as 1925, Mao turned his attention to investigation of class conditions in China. His early thinking was set forth in the pamphlet *Analysis of Classes in Chinese Society* (March 1926), wherein he sought to identify the "friends" of the revolution and isolate its "enemies." Having analyzed the conditions of the various classes, he concluded that the proletariat (to the extent to which it existed), the peasantry, the petty bourgeoisie, and the national bourgeoisie were among the friends while the landlords, the big bourgeoisie, and the imperialist agents were the chief enemies.

In 1926–1927, Mao conducted a specific study of peasant conditions in his home province and summarized the results in *Report on an Investigation of the Peasant Movement in Hunan* (March 1927). This was in effect an extension of his 1926 work, in which the role of the peasantry in the revolution was stressed and glorified. Mao saw the peasant movement as "a mighty storm," a "hurricane" that would soon sweep all forces of oppression before it. The importance of the rural areas and the key role of the peasantry remained the mainstay of Mao Tse-tung's revolutionary strategy.

From a "theoretical" point of view, then, Mao dramatized the role of the peasants. From a practical standpoint, however, he had no other alternative: a rural-based revolutionary movement has *only* the peasantry as its main force while it forms alliances with other friendly urban classes as well.

The Protracted Struggle

A rural revolutionary strategy is based on the explicit realization that, initially being weak, the revolutionaries must withdraw to secure and inaccessible but well-populated "base areas," gradually establish themselves among the local population, mobilize and win them over in greater and greater numbers, provide them with appropriate political and military training, and eventually deploy them to topple the existing regime. This process, Mao acknowledged, requires a great deal of time, patience, and hard work. Hence, the revolutionary struggle is necessarily protracted in nature.

Mao showed acute sensitivity to the political dimensions of revolutionary activity, constantly stressing the importance of political as well as armed struggle. Political activity consists, above all, of generating active sympathy and support among the country's population. The army, he said, is not only a fighting force but also a propaganda force and a working force: it must "educate" the people, help them in their daily chores, and protect them in every way. In a word, Mao called for a "people's army" to fight a "people's war."

Mao's untiring efforts to attain "unity between the army and the people" found expression in other ways as well. As early as 1928, for example, he issued (and subsequently reissued) the following set of guidelines for the army's treatment of the local population:

1. Speak politely
2. Pay fairly for what you buy
3. Return everything you borrow
4. Pay for anything you damage
5. Don't hit or swear at people
6. Don't damage crops
7. Don't take liberties with women
8. Don't ill-treat captives

From the standpoint of the revolutionaries, a protracted struggle undergoes three stages of development: strategic defensive, strategic stalemate, strategic counteroffensive. In the first stage, the main function of the revolutionaries is to retreat, protect, and consolidate their forces; accordingly, their principal form of military action is guerrilla warfare. In the second stage, the revolutionaries gradually grow in numbers and strength, eventually reaching a condition of relative parity with the forces of the regime; accordingly, when it is advantageous to them they engage in conventional warfare as well. In the final stage, the revolutionaries have presumably attained decisive military superiority over the enemy; they then confront him in open warfare. In China, this process unfolded over a period of some two decades.

In a protracted struggle, it is clear, guerrilla warfare plays a crucial role: without it, no revolutionary movement can get under way. Thus, Mao Tse-tung devoted a great deal of attention to perfecting this form of military activity. In fact, he was the great architect of modern guerrilla warfare.

Mao summarized the basic operational principles of guerrilla warfare in a deceptively simple formula: "The enemy advances, we retreat; the enemy camps, we harass; the enemy tires, we attack; the enemy retreats, we pursue."

For one thing, the entire formula hinges on timely and strategic intelligence—that is to say, clear knowledge of the enemy, his movements and activities, his strengths and weaknesses. Second, the guerrilla does not hesitate to run away (in contrast to "fighting like a man"). He insists on holding the initiative and fights only on his own terms.

Third, guerrilla warfare stresses the importance of surprise, deception, and cunning. Luring the enemy into unfamiliar and hostile territory, laying ambushes, undertaking hit-and-run tactics, striking when and where least expected—these are essential and standard guerrilla operations. Fourth, when the guerrillas decide to strike, they: (1) locate the enemy's weakest flank, (2) hit the enemy with everything they have, (3) conduct the operation decisively, surgically, and with maximum speed, and (4) disappear as quickly as possible.

Despite all this, the principal function of guerrilla warfare is not to destroy the enemy but to harass him, confuse him, disrupt his lines of communication and transportation, force him to commit mistakes, and, above all, undermine his morale. The actual destruction of the enemy takes place in the third stage of protracted conflict, through conventional warfare. Thus, in China Mao began guerrilla operations in the late 1920s and shifted to conventional warfare in the middle 1940s in order to destroy Chiang Kai-shek's military forces.

The Global Dimension of Mao's Strategy

The Chinese revolution, Mao believed, was an integral aspect of an epoch of world upheavals that began with the Russian Revolution of 1917. The October Revolution, he claimed, changed the course of world history and heralded an era of revolutionary movements around the world.

The significance of the Chinese revolution, according to Mao, lies not only in carrying forward the tradition of the October Revolution but also in its special attraction for, and applicability to, other colonial, semicolonial, and semifeudal countries. The Chinese revolution, in other words, is a new model to be followed in all developing societies where similar conditions prevail.

Taking this proposition a huge step further, Mao attempted to apply at the global level his entire revolutionary strategy. Specifically, he identified a "vast zone" of colonial and semicolonial countries that he hoped would unite to confront "Western imperialism."

The most extensive attempt to "globalize" Mao's revolutionary strategy was undertaken in 1965 by Lin Piao (1908–1971), then Mao's chosen successor. In a much-publicized document entitled *Long Live the Victory of People's War!*, Lin insisted that "Mao Tse-tung's theory of establishment of rural revolutionary base areas and the encirclement of the cities from the countryside is of outstanding and universal practical significance for the present revolutionary struggles of all the oppressed nations and peoples." He added:

> Taking the entire globe, if North America and Western Europe can be called "the cities of the world," then Asia, Africa, and Latin America constitute "the rural areas of the world." . . . In a sense, the contemporary world revolution also presents a picture of the encirclement of cities by the rural areas. In the final analysis, the whole cause of world revolution hinges on the revolutionary struggles of the Asian, African, and Latin American peoples who make up the overwhelming majority of the world's population. The socialist countries should regard it as their internationalist duty to support the people's revolutionary struggles in Asia, Africa, and Latin America.

Such is the attempt to universalize the revolutionary strategy of Mao Tse-tung. What worked in the domestic arena, it is contended, can be extended and put to work at the international level. This leaves aside the elementary problem of China's inability to control the foreign policies of other countries and dictate a common posture (or united front) vis-à-vis the imperialist powers. It overlooks the forces of nationalism within individual countries and the system of international relations that imposes constraints on what nations can and cannot do to maximize their self-interests.

THE SIGNIFICANCE OF MAO

Breaking away from the traditional boundaries of Western philosophy, Karl Marx designed a theory of revolution for advanced capitalist societies. Lenin changed, bent, and adapted this theory to czarist, semicapitalist Russia; in so doing, he established communism in Europe. Mao modified and applied the theory of Marx and Lenin to semicolonial, semifeudal China; in so doing, he established communism in Asia.

Mao's adaptation of Marxist-Leninist theory is unprecedented in its rural orientation, foundation in the peasantry, and mastery of the strategy and tactics of protracted revolution based on guerrilla warfare. With appropriate modifications, Mao's theory has been successfully deployed in such countries as Vietnam (North and South—now unified), Laos, Kampuchea (Cambodia), Angola, Mozambique, and Zimbabwe. As of this writing, it is being put to work in such other lands as Burma, Thailand, Namibia, South Africa, El Salvador, and elsewhere. The theory has not, however, had the global reach that Mao and others had hoped.

Mao's formidable contribution to revolutionary ideology and strategy must be balanced against a major personal weakness: having come to power, the methodical revolutionary sacrificed pragmatism at the altar of revolutionary purism. Specifically, Mao always remained concerned (some would say obsessed) that the mission of the revolution might be forgotten, that party and government functionaries would become entrenched bureaucrats and lose touch with the people, that feudal, capitalist, and foreign elements would resurface in China. In order to forestall such eventualities, Mao from time to time initiated mass movements of "rectification" and ideological revitalization.

The most ambitious of these efforts was the Cultural Revolution of 1965–1968. Mobilizing the Red Guards (young people who by definition embody innocence and purity), Mao shook the foundations of the party and government hierarchies. Near-chaos ensued as the Red Guards rampaged throughout the country, humiliating, purging, and imprisoning high-ranking politicians and functionaries. As events threatened to tear the country apart, the armed forces, always well organized, moved in to restore order and stability.

The process of rebuilding the party was not a smooth one, however. Internal conflicts remained widespread until after Mao's death, when the moderates finally took command. They arrested, tried, and imprisoned Mao's close associates, particularly the "Gang of Four," which included his wife, Chiang Ching. And they set out to adopt a more pragmatic posture, both domestically and internationally.

In short, as a revolutionary leader, Mao has few equals. As a postrevolutionary manager, he allowed his purism to distort his vision and judgment.

THE FRAMEWORK APPLIED

The cognitive dimension of Maoism perceives the world in terms of a dual conflict on a grand scale: (1) the struggle between the oppressed peasants and workers and the feudal lords, and (2) the warfare between colonial peoples and imperialist powers. Not until feudalism and imperialism are smashed can one rest.

The affective component of Maoism calls upon peasants and workers to unite in a victorious struggle to liberate themselves and their nation from the twin evils of feudalism and imperialism. The evaluative ingredient promises an age of peace, harmony, and plenty. Incessant appeals to nationalist values and sentiments overlap the affective and evaluative dimensions.

The programmatic component of Maoism calls for a rural revolutionary strategy, masterminded and guided by skillful leadership. A protracted revolutionary struggle begins in peasant guerrilla warfare and ends in a conventional takeover. Having applied, as he claimed, the theories of Marx and Lenin to the conditions of China, Mao had no alternative but to seek his social base primarily in the peasantry and secondarily in the workers and the middle-class nationalists. Once again, in other words, Marx's internationalism was turned into a national enterprise.

Selected Bibliography

Ch'en, Jerome. *Mao and the Chinese Revolution*. New York: Oxford University Press, 1967.

———, ed. *Mao*. Englewood Cliffs, N.J.: Prentice-Hall, 1969.

Elegant, Robert S. *China's Red Masters*. New York: Twayne, 1951.

Emi Siao. *Mao Tse-tung: His Childhood and Youth*. Bombay: People's Publishing House, 1953.

Han Suyin. *The Morning Deluge: Mao Tse-tung and the Chinese Revolution, 1893–1954*. Boston: Little, Brown, 1972.

Johnson, Chalmers. *Peasant Nationalism and Communist Power: The Emergence of Revolutionary China, 1937–1945*. Stanford: Stanford University Press, 1962.

Lifton, Robert J. *Revolutionary Immortality: Mao Tse-tung and the Chinese Cultural Revolution*. New York: Random House, 1968.

Lin Piao, *Long Live the Victory of People's War!* (Orig. pub. September 1965). Peking: Foreign Languages Press, 1966.

Mao Tse-tung. *Selected Works*. 5 vols. Peking: Foreign Languages Press, 1961–1977.

Payne, Robert. *Mao Tse-tung*. New York: Weybright & Talley, 1969.

Pye, Lucian W. *Mao Tse-tung: The Man in the Leader*. New York: Basic Books, 1976.

Rejai, Mostafa, ed. *Mao Tse-tung on Revolution and War*. New York: Doubleday, 1969.

Schram, Stuart. *Mao Tse-tung*. Baltimore: Penguin Books, 1967.

———. *The Political Thought of Mao Tse-tung*. Rev. ed. New York: Praeger, 1969.

Schwartz, Benjamin I. *Chinese Communism and the Rise of Mao.* New York: Harper & Row, 1967.

Snow, Edgar. *Red Star over China.* 1938. Reprint. New York: Grove Press, 1961.

Solomon, Richard H. *Mao's Revolution and the Chinese Political Culture.* Berkeley: University of California Press, 1971.

Wilson, Dick. *Mao Tse-tung in the Scales of History.* Cambridge: Cambridge University Press, 1977.

7

Democracy

For twenty-five hundred years, political thinkers have been concerned with "democracy" as a form of sociopolitical organization. The concept, and ideology, did not become the subject of sustained popular discourse, however, until the nineteenth century (note its association with the French Revolution in chapter two). The present century has witnessed a singular concern with democracy. Fresh attempts have been made, particularly in the postwar period, to throw light on a topic of immense complexity.

Analytically, democratic ideology has two fairly distinct features. On the one hand, it deals with certain definitional components, or core concepts; on the other, it is concerned with certain conditions deemed essential for the emergence and flourishing of democratic political order. The two aspects are closely interrelated, the conditions often being treated as integral parts of the definition. As we shall see, it is an index of the resiliency of democratic ideology that it can subsume such doctrines as conservatism and liberalism or that it can be fused with either a capitalist economy or a socialist one.

Before examining any of these topics, it would be helpful to consider briefly the evolution of democratic ideas in the West, beginning with their initial appearance in ancient Greece. The historical sketch that follows is necessarily selective, treating only the most important concepts. Moreover, the discussion excludes various conceptions of "democracy" expounded in the Eastern world because, with rare exceptions (India, for example), these concepts are predemocratic or pseudodemocratic, propagated primarily for their propaganda function. I shall return to this topic in a later section.

THE EVOLUTION OF DEMOCRACY

The Greeks

Coined by the Greek historian Herodotus (ca. 484–425 B.C.) in the fifth century B.C., "democracy" combined two Greek words: *demos,* meaning "the people," and *kratia,* meaning "to rule." Thus the original meaning of democracy was, in the literal sense, "rule of the people"; among its specific features, Herodotus included equality before the law, popular participation in decision making, and popular control of public officials.

With rare exceptions, however, other Greek thinkers did not look with favor upon democracy. Although they denounced tyranny and stressed respect for constitution and law, Greek thinkers were typically elitist—that is, they believed in the rule of the few and, presumably, the best. Plato's famous *Republic,* for instance, is openly hostile to democracy, depicting the ideal society as a fine hierarchy in which various groups of citizens perform the functions for which they are best suited and trained.

After the Hellenic period, sustained discussion of democracy became a rarity in political thought. Nevertheless, over the centuries many democratic ideas did emerge.

The Romans

Rome's major contribution to democratic government consisted in the further development of the concept of constitutionalism and in the emphasis on law as a system of norms binding on the ruler as well as the ruled. The Romans' fascination with legal matters was a consequence of their attempt to identify a concrete basis for governing the far-flung empire.

Such a basis was found in the concept of "natural law," whose principal author was the Roman lawyer, thinker, and statesman Cicero (106–43 B.C.). Although the genesis of natural law goes back to the Greek Sophists, Cicero made the concept a permanent fixture in political thought.

A series of concrete propostions will serve to summarize Cicero's discussion of natural law.

1. The cosmos is rational and governed by an underlying principle of order.
2. The cosmic process is moral and founded in supernatural reason.
3. Natural law is an expression of supernatural reason; it precedes the state and is superior to all legislation.
4. Being moral and rational, human beings can discover and comprehend natural law and govern their lives accordingly.
5. Before the law of nature all persons are equal and enjoy equal rights; natural law applies equally to all individuals because they are equally possessed of reason and equally capable of virtue.
6. Natural law endows individuals with certain rights that are "natural"; these rights precede the state because natural law precedes the state.

Cicero, in short, not only systematized the concept of natural law but also formulated explicitly, for the first time, the idea of natural rights.

The Middle Ages

The Middle Ages hold a dual significance for our purposes, one religious (associated with Christianity), the other sociopoliticoeconomic (associated with feudalism). To begin with, some parallels between Christian and Roman ideas were potentially conducive to democratic government. These included the conception of a moral law of nature, the quest for a universal society, and the belief in the dignity of the individual. Moreover, Christianity stressed, obedience to political authority is conditional, not absolute. Thus, if the ruler exceeds his earthly authority and violates the law of God, he may be lawfully overthrown.

The great synthesizer of the Middle Ages was St. Thomas Aquinas (1225?–1274) who gave natural law a distinctively religious flavor. The law of nature was viewed as the reason of God, the law of creation, the plan of divine wisdom by which the entire world is governed. It is eternal because God's rule is eternal. It represents, at the same time, participation of all rational creatures in comprehending God's rule. Human beings, by virtue of their rationality, can participate in divine providence; they must grasp the law of God and order their lives accordingly. Natural law was viewed as the final arbiter of human conduct; it applied to the ruler and the ruled alike.

Feudalism

Feudalism was essentially a series of relationships between the king, the lord, and the vassal, or serf. Too weak to control his land in its entirety, the feudal king distributed its largest portion among the lords in return for loyalty and fidelity. Each feudal unit consisted of a territorial entity in which the lord exercised complete authority. Each lord in turn divided his land among a number of vassals, thereby creating a network of interpersonal relationships. The central institution from which "feudalism" derives is *feudum,* or the fief: a grant of land by the lord to the vassal in return for services (generally, agricultural production). The vassal pledged loyalty to the lord, in return for which he was granted protection and a small portion of what he produced. This exchange of services for protection is the very essence of feudalism. Emerging from it are ideas of contract and mutual obligation. These contractual relationships were at first informal and revocable by the lord; later, they became formalized and institutionalized.

The network of feudal relationships was institutionalized in the court system, through which everyone, including the king, theoretically, was subject to law. The two types of courts, the lords' courts and the kings' courts, each emphasized trial by equals. The lords' courts were composed of a number of vassals who tried other vassals accused of breaches of contract. The kings' courts were composed of a number of lords who tried other lords. The king, as *primus inter pares,* was considered morally obliged to honor his commitments.* In case of violation or noncompliance, however, there was no effective remedy. The feudal court system has generally been regarded as the forerunner to kings' councils, representative assemblies, and parliaments.

The Reformation

The Protestant Reformation was the religious counterpart of a multitude of social, political, and economic changes all pointing toward individualism. The Reformation stressed the primacy of personal conscience and the possibility of direct relationship between man (or woman) and God. It meant, particularly for Martin Luther (1483–1546), elimination of the church as the intermediary between the individual and the Creator. It provided all people with the opportunity to interpret the scriptures for themselves.

John Calvin (1509–1564) considered salvation a question of individual effort and hard work. Success in this world, he maintained, particularly in the economic field, was a concrete indication of the possibility of redemption. Herein lies the coalescence between Protestantism and the growing capitalist economic system: Protestantism not only sanctified individual initiative and exertion, it rationalized the human acquisitive impulse into a moral duty and a calling.

---

*As the feudal lords gained in power, the position of the king was gradually reduced to that of "first among equals," and, presumably, he could be tried by the lords.

Calvinism found its most vigorous supporters in the growing industrial, commercial, manufacturing, and business classes, whose interests could best be advanced in an orderly but fairly permissive political environment and whose existence was eventually deemed necessary for the emergence of democratic government. In other words, Protestantism was congenial to the development of capitalism, which in turn was conducive to the emergence of the type of democracy that prizes individualism and liberty.

The Renaissance

The Renaissance witnessed the intensification of optimism about the future of humankind; it led to further expressions of individualism, particularly in the intellectual and artistic fields. At the core of the Renaissance was the discovery of the human being and the emphasis on self-expression, self-realization, and self-fulfillment. Only the Renaissance could have produced the "universal man," who took it upon himself to develop his potential fully and give expression to all aspects of his personality.

One of the central contributions of the Renaissance was the concept of the secular state. Its chief theoretician was Niccolo Machiavelli (1469–1527), whose main objective was the unification of Italy, a goal he believed had been undermined by the church. The major theme of Machiavelli's work is the stability and instability of political orders; its main concern is the creation of a stable, secular state.

A host of later writers, including Jean Bodin (1530–1596), Hugo Grotius (1583–1645) and Thomas Hobbes (1588–1679), further developed the concept of the state. When combined with the notion of "sovereignty," the state became a definite impediment to the development of democratic government. Sovereignty referred to the quality of final, absolute, and ultimate power in the hands of the ruler or the state. The conception of ruler-as-sovereign or state-as-sovereign fitted neatly into the scheme of monarchical absolutism.

The Seventeenth, Eighteenth, and Nineteenth Centuries

The seventeenth and eighteenth centuries witnessed serious challenges to notions of sovereignty, absolutism, and the like. The scene was England and France, and the principal challengers were John Locke (1632–1704) and Jean-Jacques Rousseau (1712–1778).* The idea of "social contract" proved to be of crucial importance for the development of democracy.

The conception of social contract involves too many subtleties and nuances to be explored through individual philosophers. Its main features were:

1. Before there ever was a government or a society, human beings lived in a "state of nature."
2. The state of nature was governed by a moral and universal law of nature, which imparted to all persons certain rights that were natural, inalienable, and absolute.
3. The state of nature offered freedoms and opportunities, on the one hand, and inconveniences and wants (for instance, common defense), on the other.
4. In order to overcome these inconveniences and wants, human beings agreed (that is, entered into a contract) to establish a governing authority.
5. Government is thus an agent of the governed, capable of doing only what it is authorized to do, such as to provide common protection and common education.
6. If the government exceeds its lawful authority and violates the terms of the agreement, it may be (indeed, it *must* be) overthrown, by violent means if necessary, but only after all peaceful remedies have been exhausted.

The idea of social contract gained immense popularity for many reasons. It was an assertion of human freedom and dignity. It was an expression of revolt against absolutism, tyranny, and monarchical rule. It was an assertion of the

---

*Though born in Switzerland, Rousseau spent most of his life in France.

consent basis of government and a justification for obedience and authority. It viewed government as a means to human betterment, not an end in itself.

The English, American, and French revolutions of the seventeenth and eighteenth centuries gave concrete reality to the social contract idea and popularized and legitimized democratic government throughout the Western world. The systematization and elaboration of democratic ideology throughout the eighteenth and nineteenth centuries were primarily the work of American, English, and French writers: Thomas Jefferson (1743–1826), Alexis de Tocqueville (1805–1859), Abraham Lincoln (1809–1865), Jeremy Bentham (1748–1832), Edmund Burke (1729–1797), and John Stuart Mill (1806–1873). The first two, together with Locke and Rousseau, are generally known as the "classical" theorists of democracy.* In the pages that follow, I shall clarify this concept and employ it as a basis for comparing earlier doctrines of democracy with their modern and contemporary counterparts.

CONCEPTIONS OF DEMOCRACY

Definitions of democracy are legion. Since it would be impossible to review—or to remember—all definitions, I shall instead group them into three types: (1) *direct, or classical,* conceptions of democracy, which have been associated primarily with ancient Greece, particularly Athens, and the New England towns, (2) *indirect, representative, or pluralist* ideologies of democracy, which emerged and flourished in the nineteenth and twentieth centuries, and (3) *participatory* democracy, which originated in the 1960s and later, a child of Vietnam and Watergate. As can be seen, analytical as well as historical imperatives characterize the three types. Each type will be examined in terms of (1) its major premises and principles, (2) the major difficulties it confronts, and (3) the implications following therefrom.

---

*Although de Tocqueville greatly admired American democracy, his personal sentiments were aristocratic, not democratic.

Direct, or Classical, Democracy

Direct, or classical, conceptions of democracy are to be found in the work of Herodotus, Locke, Rousseau, Jefferson, and de Tocqueville. Although differing in many ways among themselves, these writers contributed many ideas to the classical conceptions of democracy.

The first principle of classical democracy is self-rule: popular participation in decision making, "government of the people, by the people, for the people." A second, related principle holds that the purest manifestation of self-rule is to be found in small towns or communities. Thus, for instance, Jefferson maintained that the political organization of American society should find expression at four levels: federal, state, county, and ward. The "ward republics"—Jefferson's idealized means of self-government—were to be sufficiently small to permit personal participation of every individual in the affairs of the community. De Tocqueville's praise for grass-roots democracy was even more lavish. The town, he wrote, "seems to come directly from the hand of God." It is characterized by a high degree of "spirit" and excites "the warmest of human affections."

A third principle of classical democracy, attributed mainly to Rousseau, is that democratic government is a method of realizing the "common good" as expressed in the "common will." A fourth principle, derived from the natural law tradition, stresses the rights and liberties of individuals: "natural," "self-evident," and "inalienable," to use Jefferson's wording. Finally, all classical formulations of democracy had in common the assumption of goodness and rationality of the ordinary individual. Without this assumption, all other stipulated views would lose their significance. What, for instance, would remain of government by the people, if the "people" were not good, rational, and capable of self-rule?

The classical expressions of democracy came under heavy assault from many sources. Although there were other opponents, by far the most trenchant critics of democracy were a group of European intellectuals commonly called the "elitists" and including Vilfredo Pareto (1848–1923), Gaetano Mosca (1858–1941), and Robert Michels (1876–1936). A detailed analysis of the various attacks upon classical democracy is beyond the scope of the present chapter. I shall briefly outline, first, the general arguments against the classical conceptions and, then, the elitist critique.

The general arguments include the following. First, it was pointed out, available evidence overwhelmingly negates the notion that "government by the people" has ever been—or is ever likely to be—a reality. People, it was suggested, cannot—in the literal sense—rule themselves, regardless of the size of their communities. It has been repeatedly found that even Athenian democracy and the New England towns were dominated by minority interests.

Second, such conceptions as "common will" and "common good" are mystical, intuitive notions, incapable of demonstration and proof. There is no *one* policy, no *one* "good," that can benefit every member of a society. To be sure, such "goods" as defense and education are of general benefit, but they cannot be the distinguishing marks of democracies, because they are provided by *all* countries. In other words, it would be impossible to sort out democratic from nondemocratic government by these criteria.

Third, "natural law" and "natural rights" are assumptions neither verifiable nor necessary to political life. The validity of a natural law proposition cannot be demonstrated or tested, and there is no society in which human rights are "natural" or absolute. Fourth, liberty and equality, if interpreted in rigid and literal terms, emerge as contradictory values, incapable of attainment in any society. A moment's reflection reveals that if individuals are free, they are not necessarily equal; if they are forced to be equal, they are no longer free. Finally, it was suggested, the underlying premise of classical democracy—its faith in human rationality—is untenable, particularly in the light of findings of modern psychology.

Following up on this point, the elitists, under the strong influence of Freudian psychology, insisted that a significant portion of human behavior is motivated and sustained by irrational and nonlogical drives lying well below the level of consciousness. Human conduct is governed as much by unconscious habit as by deliberate choice.

The elitists' analysis of historical evolution established to their satisfaction that human society at all times has been characterized by a fundamental division between a minority that rules and a majority that is ruled, between elite and mass. They saw politics as perpetual conflicts among contending groups for position and power, democratic politics being no exception. In these power struggles, moreover, the elites routinely resort to myths, lies, and ideologies in order to manipulate and control the masses, rationalize and legitimize themselves, and perpetuate their rule. Moreover, the masses have a psychological *need* for leadership: lacking the necessary capabilities and skills, they *want* to be guided and ruled.

The elitists concluded, therefore, that democracy is not only an impossible and unrealizable form of government, it is irrational and undesirable as well. The masses are incompetent and incapable of self-government. The elite will always rule.

Confronted with such an overpowering critique, and recognizing the validity of much of the argument, the modern defenders of democracy set out to revise and update classical democracy in such a way as to overcome its weaknesses. The result has been a transformation in democratic thought: the emergence of indirect, representative, or pluralist democracy.

Indirect, Representative, or Pluralist Democracy

The reformulation of democracy has been the work of many philosophers and theorists—from Jeremey Bentham and John Stuart Mill in the nineteenth century to Joseph A. Schumpeter, E. E. Schattschneider, Robert A. Dahl, and Seymour Martin Lipset in contemporary times. The operating assumption of these writers is that democracy must be defined not as a constellation of idealized values but in terms of a series of propositions, practices, actions, and institutions that can be observed and verified in actual reality. The gap between the ideal and the real, as created by the classical writers, must be closed.

The starting premise of indirect, representative, or pluralist democracy is that people in a democratic society have limitations as well as capabilities. One such limitation is that they do not and cannot directly rule themselves; instead, they choose representatives and leaders who rule on their behalf.

Given this premise, the main principles of indirect, representative, or pluralist democracy revolve around the existence of many institutions, practices, and safeguards. What is needed first and foremost is the existence of political competition ("political pluralism"), understood as two or more political parties offering alternative candidates (leaders), policies, and programs. Each political party in turn coexists with multiple interest groups, civic organizations, voluntary associations, and so on ("social pluralism"). Second, people must have the ability—through elections and referenda, for example—actually to choose (as well as dismiss) leaders and programs. (This obviously requires information and education, a subject to which we shall return.). Third, it is not enough that there simply exist alternative parties and leaders; over a period of time, there must be *actual* changes in rulership (rotation in office). Fourth, parties, leaders, and governments so elected must remain responsive and responsible to the electorate: they must be answerable and accountable for their actions; they must be willing and able to meet reasonable popular demands. Finally, it is clear, such a political system cannot operate in the absence of liberty and equality—but in a relative, not absolute, sense: one person's freedom, for example, is limited by the equal freedom of all other persons.

Indirect, representative, or pluralist ideologies of democracy were variously refined and reformulated, but their essential principles remained unchallenged for a long period of time. Vietnam and Watergate changed all that by demonstrating, among other things, that a democratic government can be corrupt, unresponsive, and irresponsible.

More specifically, the "radical" and "revisionist" intellectuals of the 1960s and later launched a series of nearly crippling attacks upon pluralist democracy. Among other things, they pointed to a series of gaps between concept and reality. First, they argued, pluralist democracy claims to be objective, based on observable and verifiable facts of democratic political life. In reality, however, by stressing political competition and rotation in office, the pluralist writers express a conservative ideology of preference for stability, harmony, balance, predictability, status quo. Second, in theory pluralist democracy emphasizes political competition and popular participation, whereas in reality democratic societies are dominated and run by elites of all sorts: political, economic, industrial, military, scientific. Other than pro forma voting for *preselected* candidates, the radicals asked, what effective role do the people play? Third, in theory pluralist democracy stresses responsiveness and responsibility, whereas in reality the elites are to a large extent autonomous and beyond the reach of the public. Finally, thanks to advances in communications media, public relations, and effective "packaging," contemporary elites have vastly improved their ability to manipulate and dupe the people.

Pluralist democracy, the "radicals" and "revisionists" concluded, is a façade. The gap between concept and reality persists. What we need, they contended, is a new alternative. This alternative they labeled "participatory democracy."

Participatory Democracy

The ideology of participatory democracy is not nearly as comprehensive or elaborate as the two we have just examined. Its central premise calls for maximum popular participation in and control over candidates, policies, and programs. Or, as the slogan of the times went, "Power to the People."

Stripped to bare essentials, participatory democracy calls for at least two things: (1) decentralization of political power and decision making, and (2) direct popular involvement in political affairs. The first principle calls for devolution of power from the center (Washington) to the periphery (local communities): political decisions should be made as near to the affected source as possible. The second principle stresses the involvement of ordinary citizens in the making of these decisions. Stated differently, participatory democracy calls for the involvement of "citizen politicians" in contrast to the traditional, professional politicians.*

The exponents of participatory democracy claim a number of advantages on its behalf. To begin with, they argue, participatory democracy limits governmental abuse of power. Moreover, decision making under participatory democracy is bound to be "better"—that is, more responsive to local needs and conditions. Even if not better, it is said, the legitimacy of decisions—and hence confidence in government—is seldom called into question, since the community is bound to accept common responsibility for its own actions. Finally, in the processes of deliberation and decision making, participatory democracy provides education, learning, and enrichment for the entire community.

Problems associated with participatory democracy are no less severe than those associated with classical and pluralist ideologies. For one thing, though the radical and revisionist critique of pluralist democracy carries much validity, the suggested alternative—participatory democracy—is not a coherent ideology in its own right, being weak, vague, and incomplete. In this sense, participatory democracy was more of a *reactive* phenomenon: an outrage against the abuses of Vietnam and Watergate. For another, participatory democracy is incompatible with contemporary reality, for it overlooks the simple problem of increasing societal complexity on many fronts. How can, one is bound to ask, some of the most pressing issues of our times—arms control, the economy, pollution, poverty—be addressed at the local level? Where and how will ordinary citizens obtain the expertise necessary for handling global, national, and regional problems?

Finally, though admittedly romantic and attractive, participatory democracy is afflicted with a fatal flaw: it seeks to return to direct or classical democracy without having resolved the elemental problems that beseiged its centuries-old predecessor.

---

*The reader may remember that, taking advantage of the climate of opinion, both Ronald Reagan and Jerry Brown of California first presented themselves as citizen politicians.

On the whole, participatory democracy seeks perfection and utopia while political reality is by definition imperfect. Consequently, for all its shortcomings and flaws, indirect, representative, or pluralist democracy is the only realistic arrangement available to us today. As Winston Churchill is supposed to have said, democracy is a bad form of government—until one begins to contemplate the alternatives.

THE CONDITIONS FOR DEMOCRACY

Democratic governments do not grow in a vacuum, in any time and place, under any set of circumstances. Although the particular mix will vary from country to country, a series of concrete conditions must coalesce before democratic regimes emerge and flourish. For convenience's sake, I shall group these conditions under three headings: socioeconomic, political, psychocultural. Some of the stipulated conditions, as will be seen, are mutually contradictory, leaving it to the reader to decide the best or the most reasonable position to adopt.

Socioeconomic Conditions

The socioeconomic requisites of democracy stipulate the existence of material affluence, urbanization and industrialization, a middle class, literacy and participation, media of communication, and a network of voluntary groups and associations.

Economic devleopment—which incorporates affluence, a middle class, urbanization, and industrialization—is the most widely discussed condition of democratic government. Only in a relatively prosperous society in which a reasonably fair distribution of the national wealth has taken place can there exist the leisure, information, and education necessary to participate in political affairs. Only such a society can produce a significant middle class whose interests are best pursued in a permissive and stable environment. A middle class acts as a buffer between the extremes of poverty and wealth, and it tends to discourage extremist ideologies, whether of the right or the left.

A democratic society is a participant society in which the practice of participation is institutionalized in voting, elections, referenda, initiatives, and petitions. The evolution of a participant society, in turn, hinges on the development of literacy and media of communication.

The importance of a network of voluntary groups and associations (social pluralism) for democratic politics has been emphasized by many writers. Acting as structures of authority in their own right, groups and associations help prevent concentration of power in the government.

Political Conditions

Among the more distinctively political conditions of democracy, the following are most frequently included: effectiveness, legitimacy, an effective political opposition, and agreement (or disagreement) on "fundamentals," or "rules of the game."

Effectiveness refers to the ability of democracy to perform the basic functions of government, respond to popular demands, and provide the necessary services. Legitimacy refers to the capacity of the system to promote and retain popular support for the overall maintenance of the system. The relationship between the two is reciprocal: legitimacy enhances effectiveness, effectiveness reinforces legitimacy. Together, they ensure political stability.

The existence of effective opposition parties and groups is frequently regarded as a crucial criterion of democratic government. Some scholars, in fact, view it as *the* most distinctive feature of democracy, considering that its absence indicates the absence of democratic government. As we have seen, opposition parties and groups provide political competition and prevent monopolization of power in a few hands.

Agreement on "fundamental principles," or "rules of the game," has long been a point of contention between those who insist that such agreement is essential to democracy and those who maintain that democracy means, among other things, agreement to disagree. On the one hand, it is argued, the various components of democratic government—the executive office, the legislature, the judiciary, bureaucracy, political parties, and so on—all must play their roles in a way that is consistent with the "principles" or the "rules." On the other hand, it is maintained, any insistence on such conformity is unnecessary and undesirable; indeed, any demand for such agreement would be antidemocratic, since democracy thrives on diversity and dissent.

Psychocultural Conditions

Democratic government rests upon a "political culture" and a "political personality" that evolve over a period of time and that are virtually inseparable. It goes without saying that democratic culture and personality are markedly different from authoritarian ones. I shall briefly summarize the main contrasts.

Democratic culture and personality are receptive to divergent points of view; authoritarian culture and personality are intolerant of variety and seek to impose their own views upon others. Democratic behavior is characterized by openness to change, itself resting on a feeling of security on the part of the individual; authoritarian behavior is marked by rigidity and insecurity associated with status-ridden personalities, obsessed by fear of losing face and position. Democratic behavior integrates a variety of interests, values, and goals; authoritarian behavior is guided by rituals.

Democratic behavior is marked by "empathy": the ability to put oneself in another person's situation and see things from his or her point of view; authoritarian behavior is callous, distant, and aloof. Democratic personality is a participant personality and senses some degree of control over events and situations; authoritarian personality is a subject personality, subservient to superiors who will provide guidelines for all actions. Democratic personality is marked by the ability to play multiple roles; authoritarian personality lacks the ability to incorporate new roles and handle new situations.

In short, democratic personality is characterized by openness, security, tolerance, empathy, adaptiveness, and flexibility; authoritarian personality is marked by closedness, insecurity, intolerance, callousness, rigidity, and inflexibility.

Summary

This discussion has, it is hoped, clarified some of the conditions necessary for the emergence and survival of democratic government. Although we cannot identify a precise, uniform, and inflexible set of conditions that obtain in *all* democracies, we do know that *some* mix of conditions must prevail.

This discussion also demonstrates why, hard as we might wish, democracy is unlikely to appear in underdeveloped countries: the necessary conditions simply do not exist. A world racked by poverty, hunger, and ignorance is more likely to fall under the spell of tyrants, dictators, and juntas than democratic regimes. Thus while for political purposes from time to time the United States sets out to thrust democracy upon another country (Vietnam or El Salvador, for example), we should not expect much by way of positive outcomes.

CONSERVATISM AND LIBERALISM, CAPITALISM AND SOCIALISM

Although democratic government does not grow at any time, in any place, or under any set of conditions, it is nonetheless sufficiently flexible to accommodate a variety of ideological postures and economic systems. Thus, for instance, conservatism and liberalism have always been variants or subsidiaries of democratic ideology, even though they have undergone dramatic transformations over time.

The initial statement of conservatism by, say, Edmund Burke rested on a pessimistic view of human nature and of human ability to introduce constructive societal change. Accordingly, Burke glorified a country's tradition and called for structures of authority—political, religious, familial—to maintain order and stability. By contrast, the initial statement of liberalism by, say, John Stuart Mill was based on an optimistic view of human nature and of human reason. Accordingly, Mill called on human beings to exercise their liberty—within civilized social constraints—in order to improve their condition and bring about progress.

Over the ages, these conceptions have undergone radical changes. Specifically, in our time, conservatism has come to stand primarily for liberty and individualism; liberalism, for equality and social welfare. At times, in fact, conservatives are called "classical liberals", and liberals, "modern collectivists."

Similarly, the democratic ideology can be fused with either a socialist or a capitalist economy, thus giving us a democratic socialist government or a democratic capitalist one. "Socialism" in its *generic* sense embodies three main principles: (1) relative egalitarianism, based on the assumption of the fundamental dignity of all human persons, (2) communalism, resting on the primacy of the welfare of the community as a whole, and (3) communal ownership and control of the basic wealth of the community in the interest of the whole. Correlatively, the three core principles of capitalism would be liberty, competition, and individual (or corporate) ownership and control. Put crudely, democratic capitalism would say: "What is good for General Motors is good for everybody!" Democratic socialism would retort: "What is good for everybody had better be good for General Motors!" It is an index of the resiliency of democratic ideology that it can incorporate two contrasting sets of principles.

Socialism in its generic sense is not the same as Marxist socialism or Leninist socialism or Maoist socialism or any other kind of socialism. Marx, Lenin, Mao, and others accepted the three core principles but introduced all sorts of additions and modifications of their own.

There are actually two types of democratic socialism. The first type draws its inspiration from Marx but rejects Marx's ideas of violence and revolution, arguing, in effect, that democratic socialist goals can be achieved through gradual, peaceful means. This version of democratic socialism can be found in most European countries, especially France, Italy, and Germany. On the other hand, the second type of democratic socialism rejects Marx outright, maintaining that socialism does not need a Marxist component. This variety of democratic socialism can be found in England and Sweden, for example. Indeed, such African intellectuals as President Julius Nyerere of Tanzania and former President Léopold Sédar Senghor of Senegal take a huge step farther by maintaining that there was homegrown and indigenous socialism in Africa thousands of years before European writers formalized it into a self-conscious ideology.

THE FRAMEWORK APPLIED

The cognitive dimension of democracy perceives the world as consisting of rational and capable human beings (both the ruler and the ruled) who can live harmoniously without unnecessary coercion and force. Majority rule, representation, and constraints on government assure the continuation of this state of affairs. That not all persons equally enjoy the blessings of democracy is balanced out, in the long run, by the interests of the whole.

In its beginnings as a revolutionary ideology, democracy shared some of the same powerful emotional appeals of nationalism. It began as an outrage against tyranny and absolutism, glorifying peoples and nations instead. This is as true of the American Revolution as it is of the French. Consider, for example, the haunting appeal of the Tricolor, the Stars and Stripes, the Statue of Liberty.

As Western democracy reached a condition of maturity, however, rationalism and pragmatism overtook the preoccupation with affect, though periodically emotions make dramatic reappearances, as in the American experience with the Vietnam War and the Iran hostage crisis. Even under normal conditions, however, emotive appeal is not altogether absent. In the last couple of decades, for instance, the people of the United States have been presented with a whole series of attractively packaged and popularized promises: New Frontier, Great Society, Generation of Peace, Human Rights. And the "National Interest," of course, has been there for invocation at every whim and convenience.

The evaluative component of democracy is well encapsulated in "Liberty, Equality, Fraternity" (France) and "Life, Liberty, and the Pursuit of Happiness" (the United States). Other values are so much a part of the democratic heritage that they do not require discussion: human dignity, popular sovereignty, consent, legitimacy, obligation.

The programmatic ingredient of democracy is all too familiar to need belaboring. Briefly, democracy requires contending leaders and parties, election and representation, popular participation, education and information. It also rests on popular control to assure responsibility, responsiveness, and accountability of public officials. On a personal level, democracy calls for openness, tolerance, empathy, and flexibility.

At times, the programmatic dimension of democracy has entailed an expansionist element as well. Thus, for instance, when Woodrow Wilson set out "to make the world safe for democracy," his hope and ideal were, in effect, to universalize the values of the American civilization.

The social base of democracy incorporates the entire citizenry, except the fringe groups on the very right and the very left. Seldom, however, do we expect the "entire citizenry" to agree on any major issue. As a result, as is commonly known, democracy is a political system in which conflicting issues and demands are settled by peaceful means. Violent exceptions do take place from time to time, however, as seen in the convulsions of Western democracies in the 1960s.

Selected Bibliography

Almond, Gabriel A., and Sidney Verba. *The Civic Culture: Political Attitudes and Democracy in Five Nations*. Princeton: Princeton University Press, 1963.

———, eds. *The Civic Culture Revisited*. Boston: Little, Brown, 1980.

Bachrach, Peter. *The Theory of Democratic Elitism*. Boston: Little, Brown, 1967.

Benello, C. George, and D. Roussopoulos, eds. *The Case for Participatory Democracy*. New York: Viking, 1971.

Cnudde, Charles F., and Deane E. Neubauer, eds. *Empirical Democratic Theory*. Chicago: Markham Publications, 1969.

Connolly, William E., ed. *The Bias of Pluralism*. New York: Atherton Press, 1970.

Cook, Terence E., and Patrick M. Morgan. *Participatory Democracy*. New York: Harper & Row, 1971.

Dahl, Robert A. *Dilemmas of Pluralist Democracy*. New Haven: Yale University Press, 1982.

———. *Polyarchy: Participation and Opposition*. New Haven: Yale University Press, 1971.

———. *A Preface to Democratic Theory*. Chicago: University of Chicago Press, 1956.

De Tocqueville, Alexis. *Democracy in America*. 2 vols. 1835, 1840. New York: Alfred A. Knopf, 1945.

Domhoff, G. William. *Who Really Rules?* New Brunswick, N.J.: Transaction Books, 1978.

Downs, Anthony. *An Economic Theory of Democracy*. New York: Harper & Row, 1957.

Dye, Thomas R. *Who's Running America?* 2nd ed. Englewood Cliffs: Prentice-Hall, 1979.

Kariel, Henry S. *Open Systems: Arenas for Political Action*. Itasca, Ill.: Peacock Publishers, 1969.

———, ed. *Frontiers of Democratic Theory*. New York: Random House, 1970.

Lipset, Seymour Martin. *The First Few Nations*. New York: Basic Books, 1963.

———. *Political Man: The Social Bases of Politics*. New York: Doubleday, 1960.

Lowi, Theodore J. *The End of Liberalism*. New York: Norton, 1969.

Macpherson, C. B. *Democratic Theory*. Oxford: Clarendon Press, 1973.

———. *The Life and Times of Liberal Democracy*. New York: Oxford University Press, 1977.

———. *The Real World of Democracy*. Oxford: Clarendon Press, 1966.

Mansbridge, Jane J. *Beyond Adversary Democracy*. New York: Basic Books, 1981.

Margolis, Michael. *Viable Democracy*. New York: Penguin Books, 1979.

Martin, Rosco C. *Grass Roots*. University: University of Alabama Press, 1957.

Mills, C. Wright. *The Power Elite.* New York: Oxford University Press, 1957.

Parenti, Michael J. *Democracy for the Few.* 4th ed. New York: St. Martin's, 1983.

Pateman, Carole. *Participation and Democratic Theory.* Cambridge: Cambridge University Press, 1970.

Pennock, J. Roland. *Democratic Political Theory.* Princeton: Princeton University Press, 1979.

Plamenatz, John. *Democracy and Illusion.* New York: Longman, 1977.

Powell, G. Bingham, Jr. *Contemporary Democracies: Participation, Stability and Violence.* Cambridge: Harvard University Press, 1982.

Rejai, Mostafa, ed. *Democracy: The Contemporary Theories.* New York: Atherton Press, 1967.

Sartori, Giovanni. *Democratic Theory.* Detroit: Wayne State University Press, 1962.

Schattschneider, E. E. *The Semisovereign People.* New York: Holt, Rinehart & Winston, 1960.

Schumpeter, Joseph A. *Capitalism, Socialism, and Democracy.* New York: Harper & Row, 1942.

Weber, Max. *The Protestant Ethic and the Spirit of Capitalism.* 1904. Reprint. New York: Scribner, 1958.

Wolfe, Alan. *The Seamy Side of Democracy.* 2nd ed. New York: Longman, 1978.

PART III
RECAPITULATION

8

Comparing Political Ideologies

In chapter 1, we developed a framework for the comparative analysis of political ideologies in terms of five interrelated components: cognition, affect, valuation, program, and social base. In chapters 2 through 7, we examined the six most explosive and significant political ideologies of the nineteenth and twentieth centuries: nationalism, fascism and nazism, Marxism, Leninism, Maoism, and democracy. At the end of each chapter, we saw how a particular ideology can be analyzed, dissected, and understood in the light of our comparative framework. I shall now recapitulate our efforts by summarizing and highlighting the fit between all our ideologies and the analytical framework.

As noted in chapter 1, some overlap between the five dimensions of our framework is unavoidable. Moreover, as we have seen, nationalism and democracy share some elements of the affective and evaluative dimensions. (In fact, insofar as all our ideologies, explicitly or implicitly, appeal in *practice* to nationalist feelings and sentiments in one way or another, nationalism emerges as the most pervasive and influential political ideology of recent times.) Finally, needless to say, any attempt at recapitulation involves some repetition. But given the pedagogical objectives of this introductory text, I believe that such repetition is defensible. Nonetheless, in order to *minimize* repetition, I have decided to: (1) stress the most essential points, leaving aside much detail, and (2) lump together Marxism, Leninism, and Maoism when feasible and appropriate, particularly since the latter two are considered as variations upon the first. The entire picture is summarized in Table 8-1.

THE COGNITIVE DIMENSION

The world views of all our six ideologies involve elements of knowledge (fact) as well as of belief (fiction). Nationalism rests on the assumption of the relative superiority of one people and the relative inferiority of all others. Accordingly, a nationalist ideology seeks to establish, maintain, and enhance a country's economic, political, military, diplomatic, and cultural status.

The cognitive dimension of fascism and nazism views the world in terms of a permanent struggle involving individuals, groups ("folks"), nations, and states. In such a world, only superior power, strength, and force will prevail. Violence is not only necessary and unavoidable, it is its own justification as well.

Marxism/Leninism/Maoism perceives the world as made up of productive human beings who are everywhere and at all times exploited and oppressed for the economic benefit of a few. The resultant class struggles end in successive revolutionary upheavals culminating in a classless society in which ownership is abolished and peace and harmony prevail. Conflict, in other words, is inherent in the economic and class structures of all societies.

Democracy conceptualizes the world as consisting of rational and capable human beings who can live harmoniously without unnecessary coercion and force. Majority rule, representation, and constraints on government provide for peaceful resolution of conflicts and disagreements.

THE AFFECTIVE DIMENSION

The affective dimension of nationalism stresses the feelings of belongingness to a unique and superior group or nation. It follows, by definition, that every individual constituting the

Table 8-1
Comparing Political Ideologies

Dimensions	Nationalism	Fascism/Nazism	Marxism/Leninism/Maoism	Democracy
Cognition	Focus: country Independence and sovereignty "The best and the greatest" Superiority/inferiority	Focus: country Incessant struggle at all levels Centrality of force, power, will, strength, violence	Focus: world Creativity and productivity Primacy of economic forces: owners and nonowners Class struggle, oppression, exploitation, alienation	Focus: country Rational and capable citizens and rulers Majority rule, representation, constraints on government Flaws and imperfections unavoidable
Affect	Glorification of peoples, nations Civilizing mission, white man's burden, manifest destiny National flags, anthems, holidays	Intense nationalism Racism: biological or cultural	Moral outrage against status quo: brutalization, dehumanization "Workers of all countries unite"	Moral outrage against status quo: tyranny, absolutism, etc. New Frontier, Great Society, Generation of Peace, Human Rights
Valuation	National independence and sovereignty National pride, honor, dignity Collective welfare and security Rights and liberties Psychological catharsis	Glorification of party and state Cult of the hero/leader National pride, honor, dignity Popular obedience and submission	Egalitarianism, communalism, communal ownership and control *L'Internationale* Classless society	"Liberty, Equality, Fraternity" "Life, Liberty, Pursuit of Happiness"
Program	Asserting identity Improving prestige Dominating other people(s)	Internal: elimination of "undesirables"; improvement of condition of others External: imperialism and expansionism	Marx: spontaneous uprising Lenin: urban strategy Mao: rural strategy	Contending parties and leaders Elections and referenda Education, information, participation Responsiveness and responsibility Make the world safe for democracy
Social Base	Entire citizenry, with exceptions	Persons of racial or cultural purity	Marx: international Lenin and Mao: national and international	Entire citizenry, with exceptions

group is considered superior as well. These feelings of unity, distinctiveness, and superiority are captured in the concepts of civilizing mission (France), white man's burden (Britain), manifest destiny (America).

The affective and evaluative components of fascism and nazism overlap to such an extent that one cannot usefully separate them. Nationalism—the promised restoration of national pride and honor—is as laden with values as it is with emotions. Racism has identical characteristics.

The overriding theme in Marxism/Leninism/Maoism is outrage against the institutions and practices of capitalist societies. When combined with unceasing reminders of oppression, exploitation, and alienation this dimension provides a most potent emotional appeal.

In its beginnings as a revolutionary ideology, as we noted in chapters 2 and 7, democracy shared some of the same emotive constituents of nationalism: it began as a protest against tyranny and absolutism, glorifying peoples and nations instead. As Western democracy matured, the preoccupation with affect was overtaken by rationalism and pragmatism, except under conditions of national crisis or emergency. Even under normal conditions, however, the emotive ingredient is not altogether absent, as can be seen in the successive American invocations of such ideas as the New Deal, the New Frontier, the Great Society, human rights, and the like.

THE EVALUATIVE DIMENSION

The evaluative component of nationalism is found in the glorification of peoples and nations, popular sovereignty, individual rights and liberties. Other values include national dignity as well as collective welfare and security. In colonial contexts an additional value lies in getting even with the colonizers and righting historic grievances and injustices.

In addition to nationalism and racism, the evaluative dimension of fascism and nazism includes glorification of the state as the repository of all values. Similar attributes are associated with the party and, above all, with the heroic leader.

The evaluative component of Marxism/Leninism/Maoism idealizes egalitarianism, communalism, and communal ownership and control of the national wealth. Eventually, historical development is to culminate in an idyllic society in which all conflict ends, peace and harmony prevail, and human creativity finds fulfillment on a grand scale.

The evaluative dimension of democracy is so familiar as to require only a bare mention: liberty, equality, fraternity, dignity, happiness, consent, legitimacy.

THE PROGRAMMATIC DIMENSION

Historically, the programmatic component of the nationalist ideology has found three expressions: formative nationalism, prestige nationalism, and expansive nationalism. Thus, having become a nation overnight, as it were, France set out to increase its power and prestige by violating the rights of other peoples and nations in a series of wars that dominated the nineteenth century. Similarly, having attained independence, the United States, under the presumably divine ordination of manifest destiny, set out to expand over the entire continent and to cross the seas to take over not only Cuba and Puerto Rico but also such far-flung lands as Hawaii and the Philippines.

The programmatic component of fascism and nazism has two aspects. Internally, the regime sets out to purify the society of the "undesirable" elements and improve the condition of the "desirable" ones. Externally, it embarks upon a policy of expansionism in order to acquire fresh "living space."

The programmatic dimension of pure Marxism is weak, since it calls for spontaneous overthrow of the bourgeoisie by the proletariat. By contrast, Lenin developed a two-stage urban revolutionary strategy resting on leadership, organization, and planning. Mao masterminded a rural revolutionary strategy based on protracted conflict beginning with peasant guerrilla action in rural areas and culminating in an urban power seizure.

The programmatic component of democracy requires contending leaders and parties, election and representation, majority rule, popular participation, education, and information. It also demands popular control to assure responsible and responsive government. At times, the programmatic dimension of democracy has entailed an expansionist element as well, as in Woodrow Wilson's quest "to make the world safe for democracy."

THE SOCIAL-BASE DIMENSION

The social base of nationalism incorporates the entire population except, perhaps, the internationalists, the poor, and the indigent. In such multiethnic societies as the United States, national unity is more difficult to achieve than in homogeneous lands. Even in the United States, however, there is an umbrella ideology that brings together peoples of various regions, nationalities, and religions, and identifies them as "Americans."

The social base of fascism and nazism is necessarily limited to the loyalists: the disciplined and slavish followers of national supremacy and racial purity, especially from frightened middle classes. Fascism and nazism make systematic efforts to identify friends to be cultivated and enemies to be fought.

The social base of Marxism is, strictly speaking, international: the proletariat, regardless of time or place. (In a classless society, of course, all distinctions will presumably vanish into one united human race.) In practice, however, as we have seen, Lenin and Mao turned Marxism into national enterprises.

The social base of democracy incorporates the entire citizenry, except for the fringe groups on the very right and the very left. Seldom, however, do we expect the "entire citizenry" to agree on any major issue. As a result, as is commonly known, democracy is a political system in which conflicting issues and demands are resolved, as a rule, in peaceful ways.

CONCLUSION

This book has set forth a five-dimensional framework for the comparative study of political ideologies, examined some of the most enduring ideologies of our times, and shown how these ideologies can be broken down and understood in the light of the five dimensions.

I have stressed the importance of a comparative framework because it offers several advantages. First, a framework defines the parameters of a subject matter or a topic by specifying what is to be included and what is to be excluded. Second, and by the same token, it helps us analyze and understand a subject matter with a focus and clarity not otherwise possible: it sharpens issues and problems that may have been previously ambiguous or blurred. Third, it removes the necessity for routine memorization and the attendant boredom; once a framework is fully understood, its application becomes "fun," even exciting. Thus, if nothing else, the student of ideologies can now easily remember that, to a lesser or greater extent, all ideologies can be analyzed in the light of a set of common categories or properties dealing with cognition, affect, valuation, program, and social base. Finally, if the framework has any validity, its application extends not only to the topics or cases actually considered but to all similar topics or cases.

Accordingly, this book should be considered only a "starter" for the study of political ideologies. Having mastered the framework, and having seen some instances of its actual application, the reader, it is hoped, is equipped with the necessary intellectual apparatus for a more elaborate study of political ideologies.

APPENDIXES

A
Political Theory,
Political Philosophy,
Political Ideology

The foregoing pages have been devoted to discussions of political ideology as a concept (chapter 1), as ideologies (chapters 2 through 7), or as both (chapter 8). But as an abstraction or intellectualization, political ideology is only one part of a triad in the history of political thought, the other two being political theory and political philosophy.

For stylistic convenience, we have occasionally used "ideology" and "theory" interchangeably throughout the text. It is now time to replace stylistic liberty with scholarly precision. Accordingly, this section will briefly distinguish theory and philosophy from ideology, indicate where they converge and diverge, and point out the significance of each. Though somewhat abstract, this section is included for those who have an interest in the subject. Readers who are not interested can skip the section altogether.

POLITICAL THEORY

Were we able to (1) clarify the meaning of "political," (2) specify the meaning of "theory," and (3) successfully combine the two operations, we would presumably have an understanding of "political theory." The initial obstacle to any such attempt is the conspicuous absence of any generally agreed upon definition of "politics."

The word "politics" derives from the Greek *polis:* the small, intimate city-community. For the ancient Greeks, politics meant the science (that is, systematic knowledge) of the polis and its affairs. When Aristotle called man a political animal, what he had in mind was that man is a polis animal; that he cannot do without the polis.

Politics as knowledge of the polis meant virtually complete knowledge, for classical thought did not admit of any of the contemporary distinctions between "society," "state," "church," "community," and so on. Confusion became inevitable when "polis" began to be interpreted as city-state and, later, as just plain state. It is not happenstance that the earliest definition of "politics" was in terms of the state. The linkage with the state, however, narrows the field unnecessarily. It suggests, for example, that there is no "politics" in primitive societies or that there was none before the emergence of Western states in the fourteenth century and beyond.

More recent definitions of "politics" have been in terms of power, decision making, conflict and conflict resolution, influence and the influential, authoritative allocation of values, and the like. (I am here excluding such exotic notions of politics as Mao Tse-tung's "war without bloodshed.")

Underlying all these definitions is some conception of *order* in human affairs. What is power about—or decision making, or influence, or conflict resolution, or authoritative allocation—if not about order? This said, we confront a serious conceptual difficulty. "Order" as a criterion is not sufficiently precise to set politics apart from society, economy, religion, and so on. Put otherwise, order is a characteristic of all human relationships, not just the political ones.

One way of resolving this difficulty is to look at politics as a system of human activities conducted on two levels. At the ordinary, or common, level, there is no distinction between political order on the one hand and social or economic or religious orders on the other, for those realms overlap to a considerable extent. At this level politics and society, for instance, are one and the same. Both refer to systems of adjustment and compromise involving conflicting values and interests.

At the second, or less ordinary, level, what distinguishes

political order from other types of order is the *effective physical control* of human behavior—by means of coercion and force, if necessary. Society, economy, and the church also exercise controls—social, economic, or spiritual, as the case may be—but not physical control. In short, politics differs from society, economy, and religion only to the extent that it provides for exercise of physical force.

A definition of "theory" is somewhat easier to come by. To begin with, we must take care not to confuse "theory" with "idea" or "opinion." When in ordinary usage we say that we have a theory about this or that, what we probably mean is that we have an idea or an opinion. "Theory" has a more precise meaning.

A theory, *any* theory, consists of a set of abstractions or generalizations about reality. It refers to a series of interrelated propositions derived from recurrent patterns of human or nonhuman (for example, physical or chemical) behavior. A theory is a mental image, a summary sketch of reality as perceived. As such, theory involves simplification; it makes no claim to completeness or totality.

A *political* theory consists of a set of abstractions or generalizations about that aspect of reality that is distinctively political: a system of human activities centering upon the adjustment of conflicting interests and values that may potentially involve coercion and physical force. A political theory is an overview of what the political order is about. It is a shorthand, symbolic representation of political reality. It is a formal, logical, and systematic analysis of the processes and consequences of political activity. It is analytical, expository, and explanatory. It seeks to give order, coherence, and meaning to reality.

During the heyday of "behavioral," or scientific, political science in the 1960s, a distinction was commonly made between two types of theories: empirical (those dealing with fact) and normative (those dealing with value). As understood nowadays, political theory deals with both fact and value, both description and prescription, both explanation and valuation. Political theory, in other words, is both empirical and normative: it can offer generalizations from which value judgments may ensue.

POLITICAL PHILOSOPHY

In its literal and broadest sense, "philosophy" refers to love of wisdom or knowledge. More specifically, the major components of the discipline of philosophy have included metaphysics (ontology and cosmology), epistemology, ethics, aesthetics, psychology, philosophy of history, history of philosophy, and, indeed, even politics itself. It follows, from this strikingly broad scope, that the hallmark of philosophy is final and complete explanation of man and the universe. *Political* philosophy, to use the late English scholar Michael Oakshott's apt definition, is "the link between politics and eternity." In a word, political philosophy deals not with what is attainable but with the most lofty ideals.

Stated differently, political philosophy attempts to identify final truths. It asks final questions, and it seeks final answers. It wants to know the *highest* good, the *best* sociopolitical arrangements, the *ultimate* criterion of justice. As such, it is characterized by timelessness, finality, and universality.

This discussion gives rise to the question of the relationship between political philosophy and the normative dimension of political theory. A distinction does exist, and it hinges on a matter of relativism, a question of degree. Political philosophy deals with value judgments that are absolute, ultimate, and eternal; normative political theory addresses value propositions that are relative, contingent, and conditional. Political philosophy asks: "What is the best political arrangement for all time and place?" Political theory inquires: "What is an appropriate political arrangement for this time and place?"

POLITICAL IDEOLOGY

Given the subject matter of this book, the discussion of political ideology need not be elaborate at all. I will simply remind the reader that political ideology is an emotion-laden, myth-saturated, action-related system of beliefs and values about man and society, legitimacy and authority, acquired largely (if not primarily) as a matter of faith and habit. The myths and values of ideology are communicated through symbols in a simplified and efficient manner. Ideological beliefs are more or less coherent, more or less articulate, more or less open or closed. Ideologies have a high potential for mass mobilization, manipulation, and control; as such, they can be called mobilized belief systems.

CONVERGENCES AND DIVERGENCES

What do political theory, political philosophy, and political ideology have in common and how do they differ? The three concepts converge on the following points: (1) all involve intellectualizations, though, of course, of varying kinds and at varying levels, (2) all involve abstractions of varying degrees, and (3) all involve simplification of the universe of discourse with which they deal. The divergences are far more significant.

Political theory in its empirical dimension refers to dispassionate, disinterested analysis of political reality; its aim is description, analysis, and explanation. The normative component deals with values but in a relative and conditional manner, and as such it may serve as a basis for the making of public policy. Political philosophy begins with certain fundamental assumptions about the nature of the ultimate good. It is marked, as we have said, by finality, universality, and timelessness. Political ideology is distinguished by its emotional belief content, its mass character, and its utility in social movements.

It should be made explicit that political theory, political philosophy, and political ideology as discussed in the foregoing pages represent pure forms or ideal types. In practice, one usually encounters combinations or permutations of the three. Karl Marx is the supreme example of the theorist-philosopher-ideologue. Similarly, many political theories have a foundation in philosophy, particularly ontology (nature of reality), epistemology (nature and sources of knowledge), and ethics (nature of value).

SIGNIFICANCE

What is the importance of the various distinctions drawn in the foregoing pages? What significance does one attach to political philosophy in contrast to political ideology and political theory?

Political philosophy serves to delineate the broad goals for a society. It establishes a set of ideals against which reality may be measured. And it provides dynamism in the collective striving toward the attainment of these goals and ideals.

The importance of political ideology is at least twofold. For one thing, no political system can long endure without an accepted body of supporting beliefs among its people. For another, ideology binds a society together; it promotes individual identity and social solidarity.

Political theory provides the analyst with an abstract statement of the parameters of his or her intellectual activity. It provides the scholar with the necessary analytical apparatus for approaching his or her task. Thus, for instance, a major difference between a political theorist and a political reporter is the conceptual apparatus that underscores the former's work.

Selected Bibliography

Ashcraft, Richard. "Political Theory and the Problem of Ideology." *Journal of Politics,* 42 (August 1980), 687–705. See also the exchange with Dante Germino and John S. Nelson in the same issue, pp. 706–721, and a subsequent exchange with R. Bruce Douglas and Gary C. Marfin in ibid., 44 (May 1982), 570–585.

Brecht, Arnold. *Political Theory.* Princeton: Princeton University Press, 1959.

Cox, Richard H., ed. *Ideology, Politics, and Political Theory.* Belmont, Calif.: Wadsworth, 1969.

Hacker, Andrew. *Political Theory: Philosophy, Ideology, Science.* New York: Macmillan, 1961.

Jenkin, Thomas P. *The Study of Political Theory.* New York: Random House, 1955.

Keohane, Nannerl O. "Philosophy, Theory, Ideology: An Attempt at Clarification." *Political Theory*, 4 (February 1976), 80–100.
Lasswell, Harold D., and Abraham Kaplan. *Power and Society*. New Haven: Yale University Press, 1950.
McDonald, Neil A., and James N. Rosenau. "Political Theory as an Academic Field and Intellectual Activity." *Journal of Politics*, 30 (May 1968), 311–344.
Partridge, P. H. "Politics, Philosophy, Ideology." *Political Studies*, 9 (October 1961), 217–235.
Rejai, Mostafa. "On Keohane, 'Philosophy, Theory, Ideology.' " *Political Theory*, 4 (November 1976), 509–511.
Shklar, Judith N. *Political Theory and Ideology*. New York: Macmillan, 1966.

B
Ideology: Emergence, Decline, Resurgence

THE EMERGENCE OF IDEOLOGY

The rise of ideologies, it will be recalled, dates back, generally speaking, to the nineteenth century, coinciding as it did with the French Revolution, intensification of urbanization and industrialization, advances in transportation and communication, depersonalization and anonymity of human life, and the resultant creation of a spiritual and emotional gap. Political ideologies did not appear in preindustrial, agrarian societies for a variety of reasons. To begin with—and to state the obvious—the foregoing developments had not yet taken place (for instance, the mass base of ideology simply did not exist). Moreover, preindustrial, agrarian societies were governed by the "iron hand of tradition": near-absolute control from the top did not allow (or immediately crushed) any expression of views from the bottom. Finally, in these societies, religion was, for the most part, the functional equivalent of ideology.

Ideologies of one form or another have now dominated, with ebbs and flows and with varying degrees of intensity, the countries of Europe and North America for some two hundred years. In Africa, Asia, and Latin America, on the other hand, ideologies began to appear just after World War I and the Russian Revolution. Not until after World War II, however, did ideologies flourish in such a way as to hypnotize and mes-

132

merize the peoples of colonial and underdeveloped lands and to become the explosive forces of national and revolutionary movements.

More specifically, the Second World War and its attendant consequences breathed new life into militant ideologies in colonial and underdeveloped countries. The disintegration of the great empires shattered the myth of white invincibility: it demonstrated conclusively that in principle the white man was vulnerable. Initial Japanese military successes further showed (as had Japanese victory over Russia in the Russo-Japanese war of 1905) that the nonwhite could even *prevail* over the white.

Anti-Western nationalist and revolutionary movements mushroomed throughout Africa, Asia, and Latin America, and they were led, ironically enough, by men who had been educated in Western countries. Indeed, the genesis of many postwar independence and revolutionary movements can be traced to student and émigré groups from various colonies who met, planned, and organized in London, Paris, and other European cities and then transported the movements, as it were, to their native lands.

A related consideration in this regard is that once a colonial or revolutionary movement succeeded—once a colony attained independence—a contagion effect set in: other countries' expectations were heightened and the process of consciousness accelerated. Thus, for instance, the success of the Chinese Revolution set a formidable example for Asia, and that of the Cuban Revolution for Latin America. Similarly, the attainment of independence by Ghana in 1957 and the success of the Algerian Revolution in 1962 served as inspiration for independence and revolutionary movements throughout much of Africa.

Given the foregoing developments, it is not surprising that two ideologies, singly or in combination, have dominated the political movements of colonial and underdeveloped lands: (1) nationalism (of various forms), because it promises integrity, sovereignty, and independence, and (2) Marxism (of various shades), because it promises deliverance from poverty, disease, oppression, and exploitation. In fact, when combined, nationalism and Marxism have proved to be the most explosive political ideologies of the postwar era.

THE DECLINE OF IDEOLOGY

Some recent and contemporary developments in the advanced industrial societies of Europe and North America now warrant elaboration. To begin with, the unprecedented economic growth that occurred in these countries in the two decades immediately following World War II created an "age of affluence" (as it came to be called), accompanied by a "decline of ideology." Scholars and intellectuals undertook a series of studies subjecting the hypothesis of ideological decline to testing and verification in advanced, industrial societies. In general, the hypothesis held up quite well across the board.

The decline-of-ideology hypothesis referred to either one of two propositions: (1) a relative modulation of the ultimacy with which ideological goals were stated, or (2) a relative attenuation of the emotional intensity with which ideological goals were pursued. The hypothesis had relevance for both international and domestic politics.

Considered at the international level, the decline proposition suggested that extremist ideologies—Marxist governments, for example—had modified both their global objectives and the intensity with which these objectives were sought. When applied to domestic politics, the decline hypothesis suggested that the formerly intense competition between political parties over national policies had been moderated, that the ideologies of the left and right had to some extent coalesced into a united assault upon certain common social problems, and that there had been a relative attenuation of political cleavage and dissension.

It is necessary to be explicit as to what the hypothesis of decline did *not* mean. The hypothesis did not suggest the total disappearance of ideologies. The notion of an "end" of ideology was simply a misnomer or a misapplication. What the hypothesis did convey was an ending of "apocalyptic," "total," or "extremist" ideologies—that is to say, a decline of ideology.

This is one of the key sources of confusion in the literature on the decline of ideology, and it must be attributed in large measure to the writers themselves, who stated their hypothesis in two different ways: (1) a "decline of ideology," and (2) an "end of [extremist] ideology."

The hypothesis of ideological decline was stated within certain explicit limits: specifically, it was both time-bound and space-bound. The hypothesis was time-bound in that it embraced ideological politics in the postwar period only. It was space-bound in that it applied primarily to advanced, industrial, Western societies. The second proposition requires elaboration.

The decline hypothesis stipulated certain conditions under which it would be fully operative. These conditions had largely materialized in the industrial West, were in the process of materialization in certain countries of the East, and were largely absent in most of the developing areas of the world.

What were some of these conditions? Internationally, two developments were especially relevant: (1) a relative discreditation of the ideologies of fascism, nazism, and racism, and (2) a relative "thaw" in cold-war policies and attitudes and a relative diminution in crisis world politics affecting the superpowers.

The most important internal changes revolved around economic development and its attendant consequences: an increasing general affluence; an increasing exposure to education and the media of communication; an increasing reliance on science and expertise to solve social problems; a gradual attenuation of class and party conflict; a gradual attainment of economic and political citizenship by the lower classes; a gradual emergence of a vast, homogeneous, professional-managerial middle class; a gradual transformation of laissez-faire capitalism into the welfare state; and a gradual institutionalization of stable political processes for resolving political issues.

The decline-of-ideology hypothesis characterized not only the established parties of Western Europe and North America (whether liberal, conservative, or socialist) but their Communist counterparts as well. The Communist parties of France, Spain, Italy, and elsewhere firmly established themselves as legal and "normal" constituents of the parliamentary systems. As such, occasional revolutionary rhetoric notwithstanding, their intention was not to overthrow the system but to capture a larger share of the political pie (as in parliamentary elections, for instance).

Indeed, during the abortive French upheaval of May 1968, the student revolutionaries denounced the Communist party as a reformist organization and a defender of the status quo. They branded the party as reactionary, counterrevolutionary, and "obsolete," calling for a more radical alternative. The students' charges, by the way, were not without foundation: the party supported the student moderates and urged cooperation with university and government authorities.

THE RESURGENCE OF IDEOLOGY

The age of ideological decline was punctuated—and punctured—by a series of developments over the last couple of decades. For purposes of illustration, I will focus on the United States. The country witnessed the civil rights movement, the student movement, the peace (anti-Vietnam and antinuclear) movements, the feminist movement, the "stagflation," and the ascendancy of the Reaganites and the Moral Majority. Insofar as they bear on ideologies, however, there is nothing suprising about these occurrences.

More specifically, the charged environment of the 1960s gave rise to a variety of "radical" ideologies associated with the Students for a Democratic Society, the Weathermen, the Black Panthers, and similar groups. By contrast, the flaccid environment of the 1980s produced a group of "neoconservatives" who sought to reestablish the old social, political, military, and religious values and traditions.

In short, as the economic, industrial, and technological conditions that gave rise to ideologies in the nineteenth and twentieth centuries underwent transformation, so did the ideologies to which they had given rise. As these conditions transformed and stabilized, the ideologies in question underwent corresponding modification and modulation. By the same token, new conditions set the stage for the emergence of new and appropriate ideologies.

As with many other aspects of human life, ideologies are always in a state of flux, never remaining constant for long periods of time. Insofar as they constitute "normal" societal phenomena, ideologies will always remain with us. Understandably, "good times" tend to coincide with moderate and flexible ideologies; "bad times," with more militant and rigid ones.

Selected Bibliography

Aron, Raymond. *The Opium of the Intellectuals*. New York: Norton, 1962.

Bell, Daniel. *The End of Ideology*. New York: Free Press, 1960.

Benda, Julien. *The Betrayal of the Intellectuals*. Boston: Beacon Press, 1955.

Cox, Richard H., ed. *Ideology, Politics, and Political Theory*. Belmont, Calif.: Wadsworth, 1969.

Lipset, Seymour M. *Political Man: The Social Bases of Politics*. New York: Doubleday, 1960.

Rejai, Mostafa, ed. *Decline of Ideology*. New York: Atherton Press, 1971. (This book contains an extensive bibliography on the subject.)

Shils, Edward. "The End of Ideology?" *Encounter*, 5 (November 1955), 52–58.

Waxman, Chaim I., ed. *The End of Ideology Debate*. New York: Funk & Wagnalls, 1968.

Young, James P. *The Politics of Affluence*. San Francisco: Chandler, 1968.

Index

NOTE: This index excludes references to materials appearing in chapter bibliographies.